Plush-O-Rama

Plush-O-Rama

**Curious Creatures
for Immature Adults**

LINDA KOPP

LARK BOOKS

A Division of
Sterling Publishing Co., Inc.
New York / London

ART DIRECTOR:
Kristi Pfeffer

COVER DESIGNER:
Barbara Zaretsky

DEVELOPMENT CONSULTANT:
Nicole McConville

CONTRIBUTING WRITER:
John Murphy

ASSOCIATE ART DIRECTOR:
Shannon Yokeley

ART PRODUCTION ASSISTANT:
Jeff Hamilton

EDITORIAL ASSISTANCE:
Delores Gosnell

ILLUSTRATOR:
Orrin Lundgren
Bernadette Wolf

PHOTOGRAPHER:
Keith Wright

ART INTERN:
Courtney Tiberio

Library of Congress Cataloging-in-Publication Data

Plush-o-rama : curious creatures for immature adults
        p. cm.
    Includes index.
    ISBN 1-57990-878-0 (pbk.)
    1. Soft toy making. I. Kopp, Linda, 1960- II. Title.
TT174.3.P57 2006
745.592'4—dc22
                                    2006006334

10 9 8 7 6 5 4 3

Published by Lark Books, A Division of
Sterling Publishing Co., Inc.
387 Park Avenue South, New York, N.Y. 10016

Text © 2006, Lark Books
Photography © 2006, Lark Books
Illustrations © 2006, Lark Books

Distributed in Canada by Sterling Publishing,
c/o Canadian Manda Group, 165 Dufferin Street
Toronto, Ontario, Canada M6K 3H6

Distributed in the United Kingdom by GMC Distribution Services,
Castle Place, 166 High Street, Lewes, East Sussex, England BN7 1XU

Distributed in Australia by Capricorn Link (Australia) Pty Ltd.,
P.O. Box 704, Windsor, NSW 2756 Australia

If you have questions or comments about this book, please contact:
Lark Books
67 Broadway
Asheville, NC 28801
(828) 253-0467

Manufactured in China

ISBN 13: 978-1-57990-878-2
ISBN 10: 1-57990-878-0

For information about custom editions, special sales, premium and corporate
purchases, please contact Sterling Special Sales Department at 800-805-5489
or specialsales@sterlingpub.com.

Contents

Plush

—It's Not Just for Kids Anymore

Plush. Now what did you just think of? Incredibly cute stuffed animals oozing saccharine from their every seam? Perhaps you flashed back to a love-worn childhood bear or bunny that you snuggled up with at bedtime. Well, you're all grown up now, right? And the 30 creatures awaiting you on the following pages are not the toys of most well-adjusted children. No, they are more like what your childish imagination envisioned lying in wait beneath your bed, or hunkered in the unsettling shadows of your closet.

Welcome, intrepid friend, to a world that exists parallel to your own. Where tentacles and a third eye are the norm and not the result of artificial preservatives or a nuclear meltdown. Unbeknownst to many, there exists a fantastical world—wonderfully topsy-turvy and Seuss-like— the enigmatic world of designer plush toys.

But don't get me wrong—they are full of quirky charm. Woolie's fanged grin will elicit a smile; Polly's third eye merits a wink; and Greggle's magnificent coif of tentacles will pull at your heartstrings! Each creature marches, stumbles, and flaps to the beat of its own drummer, and I am confident many will steal your heart and make you laugh.

The designer plush toy industry is booming today with independent artists and designers armed with free time, some basic sewing skills, and boundless, unfettered imaginations. Thanks to the internet and fast shipping services, anybody who has an idea and can sew can turn him or herself into an overnight stuffed toy superstar.

We've sought out artists from both near and far, who've stepped out as plush designers and are riding high on the plush wave. As you travel through this book you'll get to meet some of them, hear where they get their inspirations, and perhaps learn a trade secret or two.

"A little background, please," you may say. "How on earth did this funky plush craze begin and how long has it been going on?" It's hard to pinpoint exactly the how-and-when the current pop-art plush toy trend began, but apparently it was the influence of Asian cartoon character designs, and a timely universal penchant for the uglier or edgier side of "cute", which spawned the aesthetic of today's plush toy craze. We do know it began fairly recently, in the late 1990s and early 2000s, and that the design ethic is bold, peculiar, and strangely compelling.

You want to try your hand at creature creation but your sewing skills are a bit rusty—or non-existent? Doesn't matter. Don't you dare let that concern hold you back. The most important tool and skill required for this art form is an overactive imagination and the courage to unleash it. This book will take you on a step-by-step plush creature creation journey, touching on necessary tools and materials, walking you through some rudimentary sewing fundamen-

tals, teaching helpful-to-know stitches (complete with illustrations), and giving tips on how to customize your own creation through fabric selection and simple embellishments.

So welcome to the new plush frontier where it's perfectly acceptable to be a bit quirky, where unabashed originality is highly encouraged, and "not-quite-right" is the norm.

Creature Creation

You wouldn't believe what a release it is to actually construct your inner child—or personal demon, out of fabric and stuffing. It's cheaper than therapy and gives you something to sit on your couch when you're done. Use the basic procedures that follow to create the creatures in this book or to bring your own imaginary friends to life.

BASIC MATERIALS AND TOOLS

You're most eager to begin playing Frankenstein and start making a creature that caught your eye while thumbing through this book—and understandably so! But once you get started and are elbow-deep in stuffing, you won't want to stop what you're doing to run out to the store to pick up a scrap of fabric or a forgotten notion. Go ahead and take the time to gather all the supplies you'll need to complete your monster from beginning to end. There's a basic set of tools that you'll need for every project.

Basic Creature Tool Kit

Scissors (ideally both fabric and craft)

Straight pins

Sewing machine (optional)

Sewing needles and coordinating threads

Polyester fiber stuffing

Wooden spoon, dowel, or unsharpened pencil (to aid in stuffing and helping to turn the fabric)

Fabric of your choice

Almost any fabric will do. Fleece, felt, faux fur, and material from recycled clothing are among the fabrics recommended for the projects in this book. Browsing through thrift shops and rummaging through yard sales may result in the perfect fabric find that fully expresses your creature's inimitable personality. Repurpose a friend's, child's, or a well-worn favorite garment of your own to make a creature with special nostalgic meaning.

If your fabric has some stretch to it, you might find it easier to stuff, and more forgiving when turning your sewn creation right side out. A little stretch will offer some unpredictability as to the final shape and dimension of your item, but will only serve to make your creature even more uniquely yours.

8

100% wool sweater swatch

Same swatch as above, after being felted.

CREATING FELTED WOOL FABRIC

You'll find that several designs in this book are made with felted wool fabric. Felted wool has a lot going for it. It's sturdy, doesn't ravel, and has a wonderfully rich texture. Felting vintage sweaters from your local thrift shop ensures a one-of-a-kind look.

Selecting a Sweater to Felt

The felting process will drastically shrink a sweater, so purchase one that is a men's sized medium or larger.

Choose sweaters made of 100 percent wool. One hundred percent lambswool, cashmere, and wool/angora blends also work, but may require multiple runs through the washing machine. You can also felt sweaters made from a wool blend containing less than 10 percent acrylic/nylon fiber. Remember, the bulkier the knit, the rougher and thicker the felted fabric, so bear in mind your sewing machine's (or your own fingers'!) capabilities, and the desired 'cuddliness factor' of your finished plush when choosing sweaters to felt.

The Felting Process

Remove any zippers and buttons before beginning the felting process.

1 Using the hottest setting on your washing machine, add the sweater(s) and some liquid laundry detergent. Allow the item(s) to run completely through the cycle.

2 Once the machine finishes the complete cycle, check the felting process. If the garment stretches easily, or the stitches are still readily visible, you will need to repeat the process, in some cases perhaps several times.

3 Once the item is sufficiently felted, hang it up to dry. The sweater will be quite tiny! The dryer can hasten felting, but on regular wool it also results in adding a significantly rougher feel to the fabric. You might want to consider the dryer only when felting cashmere. If you do decide to use the dryer, remove any items promptly.

Be forewarned that after the felting process, your washing machine will be full of lint. Wipe the interior drum with a damp cloth before adding any other laundry.

Once you have a tiny, dry, felted wool sweater, you will want to turn it into pieces of felted wool. Cut the felted sweater into four pieces by first removing the arms at the shoulders, and then cutting the front and back of the sweater into two separate pieces. Work along the existing seams. You may need to turn the item wrong side out to see the seams.

Sharp fabric scissors

Find these at a craft or fabric store. They might be an investment cost-wise, but will prove to be a good one. Sharp, quality, scissors will last a long time and will make a noticeable difference when cutting all types of fabric. Use craft scissors when cutting paper as using your fabric pair will quickly dull them.

Sewing machine or sewing needles

Sewing machine needles come in different sizes, and can be purchased based on the weight and texture of the fabric you'll be working with. If you don't want to buy fabric-specific needles, you can take the easy route and use a universal needle. These typically come in packs of four or five. Buy several packs as they're not too pricey, because you'll surely break a needle from time to time, especially if you're sewing through thick or multiple layers of fabric. Also, sometimes if you catch a pin while you're sewing, your needle will break and you'll have to replace it.

While more time-consuming, many of the patterns in this book may be sewn by hand. If you choose this path, a variety pack of hand needles will suit you for most purposes. This will include some general sewing needles, often called sharps, some embroidery needles, and some darner's needles. You might also try some milliner's or straw

needles, which are longer than average and easy to handle. Choose a needle based on the weight of your fabric and the purpose of your stitching. Thicker fabrics often require thicker, longer needles. You be the judge of what you need for your project.

Sewing machine or no, any plusher must have a set of doll needles in his or her arsenal. These are thick, sturdy needles with gracious eyes, and are used for soft sculpting an already-stuffed item. These do what regular hand-sewing needles cannot by having the length to stitch through vast expanses of stuffing and fabric.

Thread

We beg, urge, and implore you to stay away from that horrid garbage in the four-spools-for-a-dollar bin. That stuff will snap quicker than a spider web on the flats of Tornado Alley. Although pricier, invest in some good polyester thread for your sewing machine and basic hand sewing. This thread has some strength to it, while being light and thin enough to pass through fabric with ease.

For hand stitching and attaching features like buttons or beads, upholstery thread and even carpet thread is recommended. Upholstery thread is nice and smooth and, while being thick and sturdy, is snag-free. You'll love it. Carpet thread is thick and will hold your seam or sewn-on item with unmatched strength. Use it with a doll needle because the eye is big enough to accommodate such a hefty thread.

Many a plush creature may benefit from a touch of embroidery. Use embroidery thread to sew a quizzical eyebrow, an impish grin, or a bit of chest hair.

Straight pins

Short metal pins with tiny heads will do the job, but longer ones with big, round, plastic or glass heads are easier to handle, and much more visible when it's time to remove them. When giving your creature a big squeeze, nothing ruins the bonding experience like discovering a stray pin. Avoid this unpleasantry by using a pin that can be seen with greater ease.

Seam ripper

These little wonders are as much a necessity as a pencil eraser. Even the most adept seamstress will wind up stitching something inside out or just badly, and need to pluck the thread out for another try. A seam ripper makes quick work of the task.

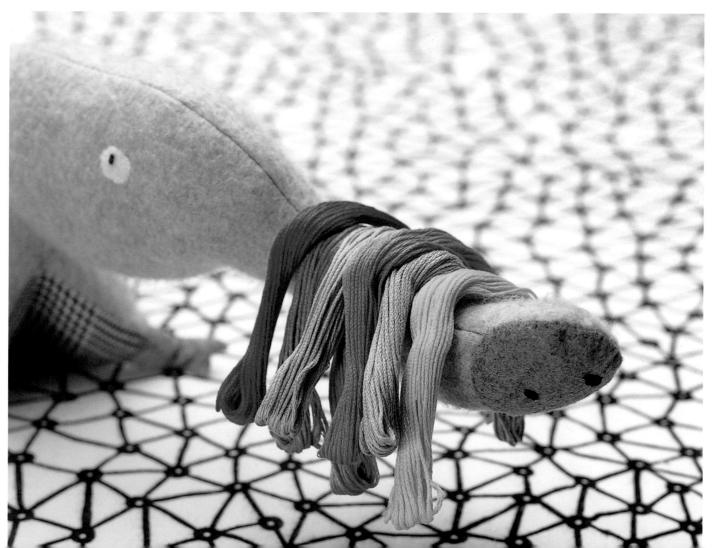

Types of Stuffing

Polyester stuffing is recommended for its washing and drying ease. It keeps its shape and distribution within a plush item even after a trip through the dryer.

Grade one stuffing is brand new, soft, and fibrous. It's resiliency and non-allergic qualities make it ideal for creature stuffing. You can readily find this type of stuffing in any fabric or craft store in quantities ranging from 12 ounces to bulk cartons.

Grade two polyester stuffing has an inherent coarseness, causing it to have a bit more bounce than its brand-new counterpart. It's a wonder, nicely filling out plush items with few lumps and nodules, plus the added bonus that it's environmentally friendly. If interested in this type of stuffing, be prepared to make a serious commitment, as it is only available in bulk quantities. Ask your craft or fabric store if they carry such a product.

If you'd like to endow your plush creation with the ability to sit up, you may opt to stuff some areas with polypropylene pellets. These pellets will add weight to your plush and allow for some lifelike posing, such as leg-crossing. Experiment with a combination of pellets and polyester fiber to reach the desired effect. Remember that a toy with this type of stuffing is not suitable for young children.

Embellishments

This is where you can really go crazy-creative. It's a wonder how the simple addition of a couple of buttons or the incorporation of a bit of vintage trim can completely transform your plush's personality. Consider shirt collars, feathers, fancy trims (often available by the foot or yard off of a spool), jingly bells, ribbon, pants pockets, or any reusable portion of a fabric item that's seen better days.

Eyes

The type of eyes and whether your plush has one, two, or three of them is vital to its facial expression. Your options include buttons, child-safe doll eyes, stitching, or other materials of your choosing.

Child-safe doll eyes are available at some craft stores but often have to be ordered from doll part suppliers. These eyes come in many shapes and colors, and have a plastic shaft on the back of them that pokes through the fabric and fixes on with a clamping washer. They stay on incredibly well and cannot be chewed off by newly cut teeth, or by most people who like to gnaw on things.

These eyes are highly recommended if your plush items will be marketed to the general public or might wind up in the loving arms of anyone under three years of age.

Buttons are just nice. They're economical to buy, simple to sew on, and make great eyes. You can find them in a myriad of colors and shapes at fabric and craft stores. Do not use buttons if the intended recipient of your plush is under three years of age.

SEWING 101

If you're an accomplished seamstress you may pick up a few hints by breezing through the following sections. Conversely, if the process of sewing a button back on is a mysterious and intimidating one, or if you're a little foggy on sewing terminology, there are some basic terms and techniques you should familiarize yourself with before getting started. Refer back to this section as needed.

Right sides together

As you arrange your pieces of fabric to sew them together, always place them with their "right sides together," or in other words, laying them with the "pretty" sides facing each other. You want to sew on the wrong sides so that your seam will be hidden when the piece is turned right side out again. Of course, if the aesthetic of your piece involves letting your seams show, then by all means, arrange your fabric with the wrong sides together. Seams ought to be hidden though, especially if a fabric is woven or knitted and has the potential to unravel. Fabrics like felt or fleece don't have this potential.

Pinning

You should pin where corners meet and wherever you intend to sew a seam. To pin properly, use the very tip of the pin. Match the edges of your fabric that you intend to stitch (right sides together). Send the pin's tip through both layers of fabric about 1/4 inch from the fabric's edges. Push the pin's tip back up through both layers of fabric, exiting around 1/16-inch from your original entry point, perpendicular to the fabric's edges. You don't need to use the entire length of the pin; in fact it's best if you don't. Pinning with just a tiny portion of the pin ensures a truer alignment of your fabric.

Seam Allowance

Seam allowance is the distance between your seam and the cut edge of your fabric. Its purpose is to assure that your needles catch the threads of the two fabrics you're joining, especially if your fabric is prone to unraveling. A 1/4-inch seam allowance is standard for most plush toy projects and fabrics, but can vary. Essentially, if the weave of your fabric is loose, or has the potential to unravel, sew perhaps 5/8-inch or more in from the edge. If your fabric is tightly woven and has no potential for unraveling, your seam allowance can be narrower if you want.

Assembly

Many times arms, legs, horns, and appendages such as tails and tentacles are sewn right into the seams when the right sides are together, and before the whole assembly is turned right side out. In this state, your toy will only vaguely resemble that of the finished creature. Appendages are positioned so that they are facing inward, sandwiched between the two facing right sides of the fabric. Pin them securely in position, making sure that at least 1/4 inch of the appendage will be caught when the seam is sewn.

14

Notching

When sewing a tight turn, for instance up one leg and down the other, you'll leave a seam allowance. When you turn your item right side out again, you'll notice the turn you've just sewn looks bunched up. You can prevent this ghastly occurrence by notching the seam allowance at the turn before you turn your plush right side out. To notch, simply cut little 1/8-inch Vs in the seam allowance along the curve or turn, from the edge of the fabric almost to the seam. This will relieve the tension on the seam allowance which causes bunching when turned right side out. You can achieve the same objective by cutting little slits in the seam allowance. Either way, you'll want to make several notches or slits to assure a smooth turn.

Stuffing

Take the time to stuff your item properly. Exercise patience when doing this. Use small pieces of stuffing, especially where the space to be stuffed is small—and never cram. For stuffing narrow places where fingers cannot reach, use a 1/4-inch wooden dowel with a roughened end, the handle of a wooden spoon, or an unsharpened pencil, to gently and deftly guide bits of stuffing. Using small pieces of stuffing helps prevent lumps or hard nodules.

Be gentle, and don't pop any seams with excessive stuffing force. Stuff as firmly as your piece needs to maintain its shape and integrity without overstuffing.

USEFUL STITCHES

Even if you're utilizing a sewing machine, many of these creatures will require some level of hand sewing, whether decorative in nature or to attach appendages and embellishments. The following section describes how to make the basic stitches recommended in the instructions, and explains the specific use for each.

Stitching By Machine

Using a sewing machine to stitch your creature together is both a labor and timesaver. While some hand stitching may still need to be done, in many cases it will be minimal. The following stitches will help ensure professional-looking results.

Back Tacking

Back tacking is a sewing machine method for securing the beginning and the end of a stitch. This is the machine equivalent of tying a stitch off by hand. To back-tack, stitch forward two or three stitches, reverse-stitch the same amount, then continue forward over the top of all the stitches you just made. Some would say the back tack punctuates your seam, and whether or not it does exactly that, professional quality is ensured.

Basting

The basting stitch is essentially the same as the straight stitch, except with your machine set on the longest stitch length. Use this stitch when you want to hold two pieces of fabric or other material together temporarily.

Straight Stitch

The straight stitch can be used for topstitching, seaming, and basting. Set your sewing machine to perhaps 2 or 3 in length, with 0 for the width. Your machine achieves this stitch by drawing a top thread through the fabric, then looping it with the bobbin (or bottom) thread.

Zigzag

The zigzag stitch is an attractive way to attach felt facial features, and is also useful if you have a raw edge that you want to bind to prevent it from unraveling. Unraveling can also be avoided by leaving enough seam allowance.

Stitching By Hand

If you don't own or have access to a sewing machine, but have the time and inclination, all the creatures in this book may still be successfully created with a simple needle and thread and a few of the stitches outlined below.

Backstitch

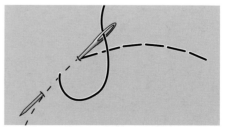

The backstitch is a hand-stitching method for creating a seam. It's a good stitch because it allows for greater ease when stuffing. To make this stitch, enter your fabric with your needle from behind the two layers you want to join. Bring the needle all the way through. Send your needle back through both layers as you would a basting or running stitch. Reenter with your needle as you did originally, but backwards, half the length of the original stitch, coming up through the middle of your original stitch. Pull your thread taut, and make a stitch the same length as the previous one, reentering the fabric at a point beyond the end of your original stitch. Your stitches on the underside will be twice as long as those on the upper side. Repeat this process until you have completed your seam.

Basting Stitch

Basting is a means of temporarily securing two edges of fabric where a seam is intended to go. Based on the straight or running stitch, this particular stitch is exactly the same except it is sewn in exceedingly long lengths.

Blanket Stitch

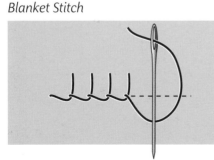

The blanket stitch is a decorative technique for accentuating an edge, or for attaching a patch or cut shape to a layer of fabric.

With your thread at the edge of your fabric or patch, poke the needle through the fabric at a point in a vertical line above the fabric edge. Make a straight downward stitch with the thread running under the needle's point. Pull to form the stitch.

Ladder Stitch

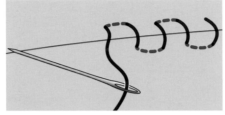

The ladder stitch is used for attaching limbs and appendages, as well as for closing up a stuffing hole in such a way that your stitches are hidden and the seam allowance remains inside. This method is sometimes referred to as "stitching in the ditch." Make your first stitch perpendicular to the seam, piercing both pieces of fabric. Next, make a small running stitch along the length of the seam. When the thread is tightened, the stitches should be virtually invisible.

Straight Stitch

This stitch is as basic as it sounds. Used for sewing woven fabrics together, it is the most fundamental and most important. In the case of hand sewing, a single thread is drawn in a straight line through the front side of the fabric and then back down through, thereby bonding two pieces of fabric together.

Tacking

Tacking is a temporary means of securing two layers of fabric together at a single point with a small stitch. Some people call these Tailor's Tacks.

Whip or Overcast Stitch

The whip or overcast stitch is a hand stitch used for binding edges to prevent unraveling. It's quite easy. Just stab your needle through your fabric, roughly $1/8$ to $1/16$ inch from the edge, and pull it out the other side. Loop the thread over the fabric's edge and reenter on the same side of the fabric you entered before, as close as you can to your original point of entry, roughly $1/16$ inch or closer. Send the needle all the way through and repeat the process. If the stitches will be purely decorative in nature, you may make them farther apart.

CUSTOMIZING

Once you have a plush or two under your belt and feel comfortable in your ability, we encourage you to use the designs in this book as points of inspiration. Templates for some of the more complex plush projects are provided. Actual dimensions for each project are given in the instructions, but don't feel obligated to create your plush in that size. Part of the creation adventure is enlarging the pattern pieces to whatever size will produce the creature of your heart's desire. Somewhere along the way, depart from the written instructions and let your creature take on a persona all its own. Utilize a basic pattern shape, but add some fur, feathers, or maybe an extra limb or two, like Mr. Potato Head gone terribly wrong. Let a needle and thread and a googly eye or two set your inner self free.

16

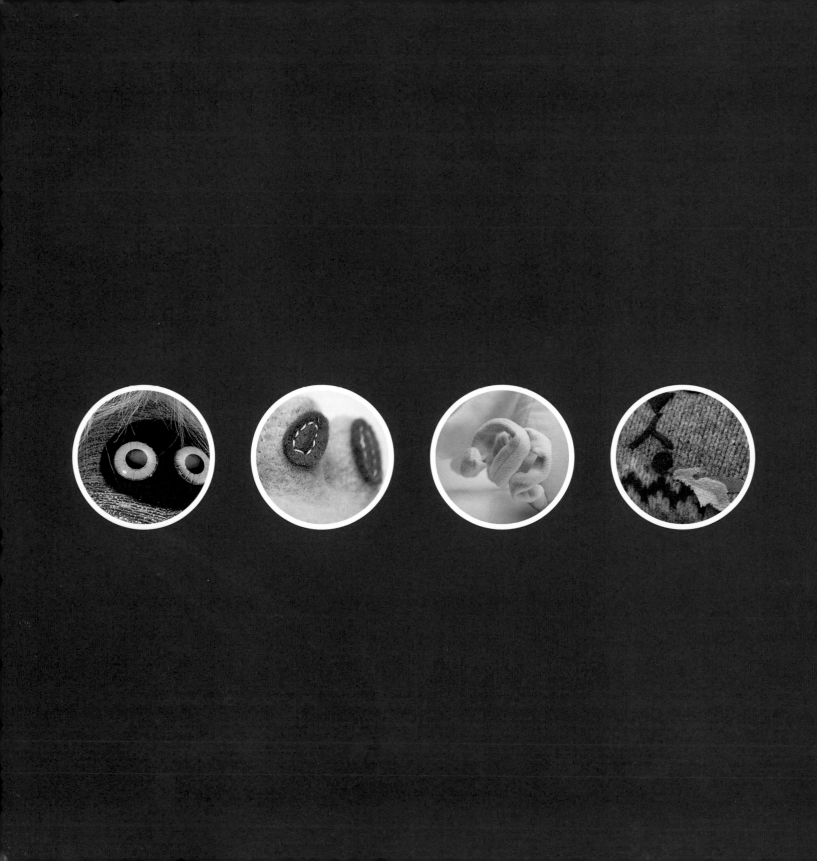

We cyber-trotted the world 'round to bring you representatives of the fascinating plush population. Our tireless efforts were rewarded as a procession of plush curiosities hopped, flew, walked, swam, crawled, and slunk to be interviewed and photographed for this book.

Most felt honored by the recognition, although a few were a bit puzzled, and one was frankly annoyed, but in the end they all graciously gave us exclusive glimpses into their lives and personalities—which you'll likely find to be as unique as your own. Don't be surprised if some of their quirky characteristics remind you just a tad of someone you know...

So with no further a-do, prepare to

Meet
the Creatures

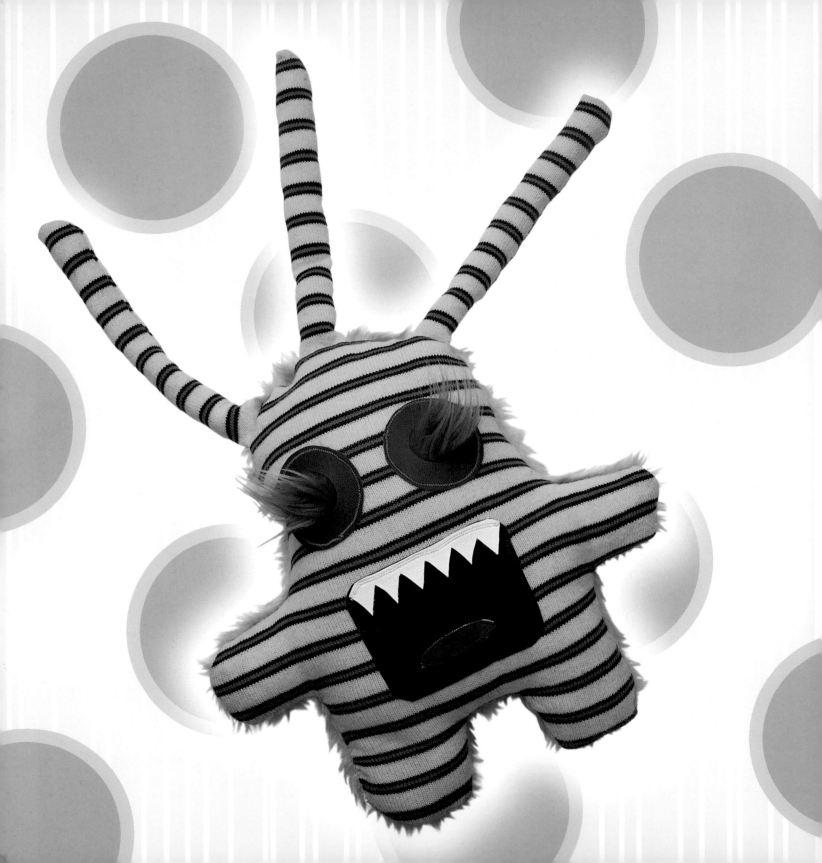

Greggles

Born during a violent thunderstorm, Greggles enjoys eating butterflies, hugging strangers, and dancing in the dark. He is happiest when he sees people crying as they laugh.

Stuff You'll Need

Striped material

Short fake fur

Long fake fur

Black, red, white, and purple vinyl

Tailor's chalk

FINISHED PROJECT SIZE AS PICTURED IS 11 X 11 INCHES (NOT INCLUDING TENTACLES).

How to Create Greggles

1 Using the photograph as a guide, draw or trace, and then enlarge and cut out the pattern pieces. Trace around and then cut out the following pieces: one body half from your chosen fabric, and one body half from the short fake fur, long fur for the eyes, and vinyl for the donut-shaped eye covers, teeth, mouth and tongue.

2 To create the three tentacles, cut out three rectangles of fabric.

Fold each fabric rectangle in half length-wise so the right sides are facing, and pin.

3 Start the stitching in the folded corner of the fabric, curving around to sew down the length of the tentacle. Leave the other end open (figure 1).

4 Turn the tentacle right side out. You may stuff the tentacle with a small amount of stuffing if you'd like, or none at all. The less stuffing, the floppier the tentacle.

5 Sew the face parts onto the front body half. Use pins to hold the pieces in place as you sew. For the eyes, cut the long fur in a circular shape small enough to fit under the eye covers, but larger than the holes in the eye covers (figure 2). Position and sew the long fur in place. Place the donut-shaped eye covers over the fur, and pull the eye fur through the center hole. Finish by sewing around the outside of the donut shape.

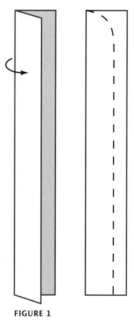

FIGURE 1

FIGURE 2

long eye fur

donut shaped eye cover

DESIGNERS: **DARREN FRISINA** AND **ESTHER WAIN**

6 With the face sewn onto the front half of the toy, pin the two halves of the body together with the rights sides facing inwards. Pin every ¹/₂-inch along the outside of the body. Pin the tentacles in place on top of the head, with their length extending into the toy, and with their open ends facing out (figure 3).

7 Sew around the outside of Greggles, leaving a gap to turn him right side out, preferably along a straight section on the leg to make it easier to stitch closed.

8 To ensure the toy lies flat when turned right side out, snip each corner of the toy near the arms and legs without cutting the stitching (figure 4).

9 Turn Greggles right side out and stuff with polyester fiber. Finish by hand-stitching the hole in the body closed.

22

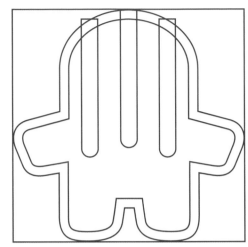

FIGURE 3

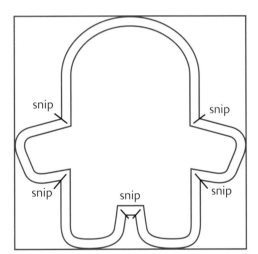

FIGURE 4

Reg

Despite his scary teeth, Reg is all heart. He lives in a tent with Claude, his pet mouse. They make regular trips to the seaside.

Stuff You'll Need

Tailor's chalk or pencil

Bright fabric

Felt (for eyes, teeth, claws, spine, and horns)

Thread in a contrasting color to your fabric

FINISHED PROJECT SIZE AS PICTURED IS 4 X 8 INCHES.

How to Create Reg

1 Using the photograph as a guide, draw or trace, and then enlarge and cut out the pattern pieces. Pin, trace around, and then cut two body pieces out of your chosen fabric.

2 Cut the mouth and eyes out of felt, position them on the front body piece, and sew around the edges. Stitch the teeth in a zigzag pattern, using the photo as a guide.

3 Cut out the horns. You will need to cut four. Sew two of them together around the edges, leaving the straight edge open, and then turn right side out. Repeat with the other two pieces.

4 Cut out four arm pieces and two felt "claw" pieces. Place two arm pieces so the right sides are together. Sandwich a felt claw at one end of the arm, between the arm pieces. Sew around the edge leaving the top edge open (figure 1). Turn right side out and cut the brown felt to create the zigzag claws (figure 2). Repeat for the other arm.

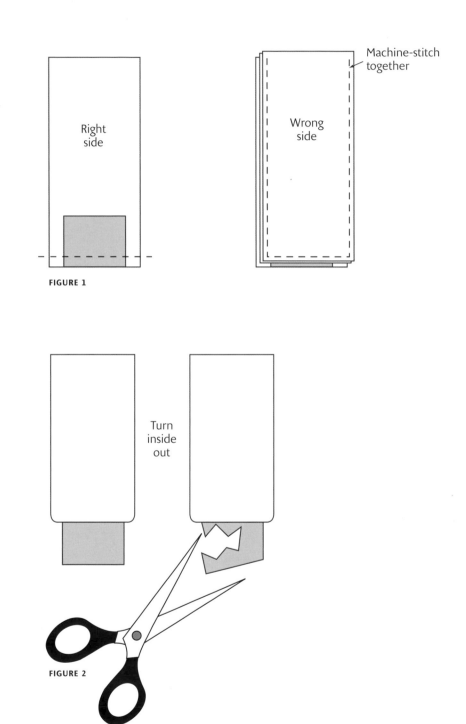

Right side

Wrong side

Machine-stitch together

FIGURE 1

Turn inside out

FIGURE 2

DESIGNER: **KATE SUTTON**

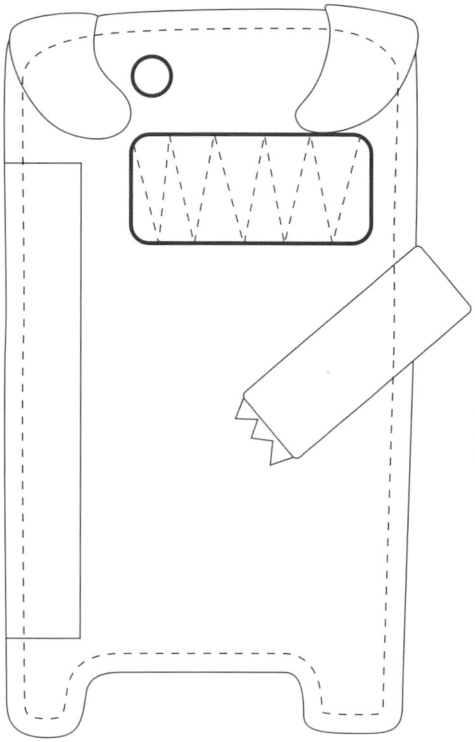

FIGURE 3

5 Place all the pieces together, as shown in figure 3. Be sure that the right sides of the body pieces are facing each other. Tack everything in place.

6 Sew the front and back together, leaving a 1½-inch gap open to turn Reg right side out; stuff with polyester fiber. Hand-stitch the opening closed.

7 Sew the end of the other arm closed. Use a ladder stitch to attach the arm to the body. Cut the spine felt to create zigzag ridges (figure 4).

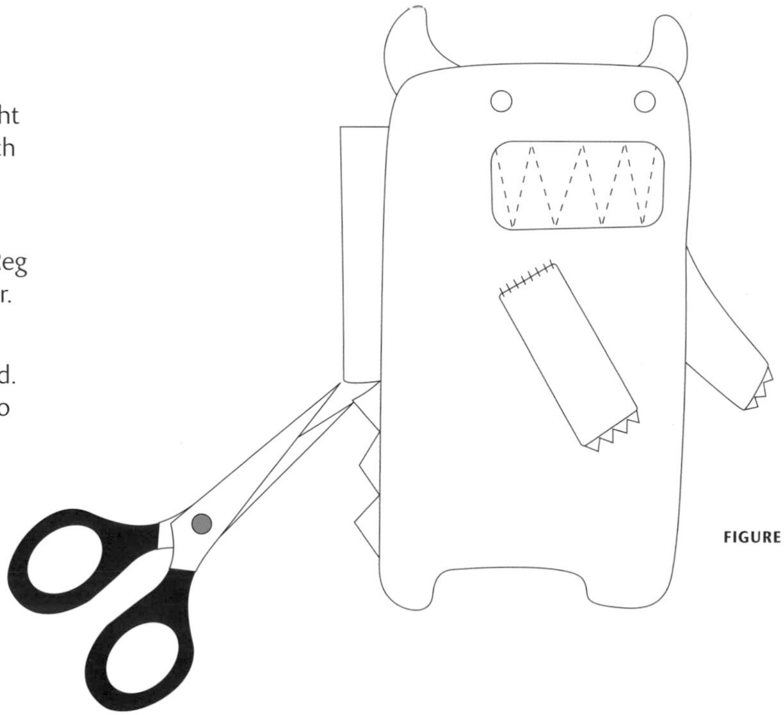

FIGURE 4

Monkey in the Middle

Monkey in the Middle is a retired world heavy-weight champion wrestler. At the pinnacle of a match, he would use his beefy forearms to perform his signature headlock on his overwhelmed opponents. Always with a head for business, Monkey prudently squirreled away his winnings and now owns a chain of fast-food restaurants in Buffalo, New York.

Stuff You'll Need

Faux fur

Brown wool felt or other medium-thickness fabric

White and black felt (for eyes and fingers)

Embroidery needle

Black and white embroidery floss

FINISHED PROJECT SIZE AS PICTURED IS 5 X 12 INCHES (BODY ONLY).

How to Create Monkey in the Middle

1 Using the photograph as a guide, draw or trace, and then enlarge and cut out the pattern pieces. Pin the body piece to the fur and cut two. Pin the rest of the pieces, except for the fingers and eyes, to the wool felt and cut two of each, leaving a ¼-inch seam allowance.

2 Start by sewing all the fingers together, then stuff and sew them closed. Set them aside to attach to the arms later on.

3 Sew the arms together, leaving openings to insert the fingers. Pin the fingers in place, and hand-sew closed. Stuff and set aside.

4 Sew the legs together, leaving the top open. Stuff, and then sew them closed. Set the legs aside to work on the face.

5 Use your favorite embroidery stitch (chain stitch, backstitch, or satin stitch) to embroider Monkey's nose and mouth onto the felt face area. Do the same on white felt to make the eye pupils. Attach the eyes to the face.

6 Embroider inside the front of each ear, or machine-stitch some circles on it. Sew with the right sides together, leaving the base of the ear open. Turn the ear right side out, and insert a little stuffing or a circle of batting inside the ear to give it some rigidity.

7 Sandwich the ears facing inward between Monkey's two head pieces, so their bases will be caught in the seam during sewing. Make sure that his face and the right side of the fabric for the back of his head are facing each other.

Pin around the head, leaving an opening for stuffing and turning. Sew together all the way around, except for the gap area. Turn right side out, and the ears will pop into place. Stuff, and sew the head closed.

8 Sew the two body pieces together, leaving openings to insert the arms and legs. Turn the body right side out and stuff. Insert the arms and legs in place, and then hand-stitch to secure. Attach the head to the neck using a ladder-stitch.

DESIGNER: **LIZETTE GRECO**

Mr. Skelly

Mr. Skelly is known for his clever dance moves and his love of edamame. He's most pleased when all the Halloween and Day of the Dead decorations are packed away, leaving him space to practice his elaborate dance routines.

Stuff You'll Need

Tailor's chalk

Medium-weight black fabric (a fabric with a little stretch is best)

White felt

FINISHED PROJECT SIZE AS PICTURED IS 6 X 11¼ INCHES FOR THE BODY. ARMS AND LEGS ARE EACH 5 INCHES LONG.

How to Create Mr. Skelly

1 Using the photograph as a guide, draw or trace, and then enlarge and cut out the pattern pieces. Pin the body, arm, and leg patterns to the black fabric. Trace around each with tailor's chalk. Cut the pieces out and set aside.

2 Pin the "bones" patterns to the white felt. Cut out the eyes, teeth, and nostrils details using sharp fabric scissors.

3 Pin the white felt bone pieces to the right side of one of the black body pieces.

4 Use a sewing machine, or hand-stitch the white felt to the black fabric using straight stitches. Don't forget to stitch around Mr. Skelly's eyes. If desired, you can stitch a smile over his teeth, or leave it the way it is.

5 Sew the seams of both arms and both legs. Turn them right side out when finished. This part can sometimes be frustrating. Take deep breaths.

6 Stuff the arms and legs with polyester stuffing. Sew the open end of each arm and leg closed, and then set aside.

7 Place the body pieces with right sides together, and pin. Sew around the edges, leaving areas for the arm and leg holes open, as well as a 3-inch opening between the left arm and leg hole.

8 Turn the body right side out. Insert the finished arms and legs into their respective openings, and stitch closed. Mr. Skelly loves this part!

9 Fill Mr. Skelly's head and body with poly stuffing. His neck will require a lot of attention. Make sure the stuffing fills out the finished shape, but doesn't overflow. Mr. Skelly is very physically fit.

10 Stitch the opening securely closed. Voilà! Bring on the edamame.

DESIGNER: **LEYA WILLIAMS**

Polly is a tea party hostess from a distant planet. Everyone there serves tea for a living, but none so nicely as Polly. She attributes her success to her red striped stockings. Beware of her tea cookies, however; just one of those will make you silly for up to 60 days.

Stuff You'll Need

Green cotton or corduroy fabric

Recycled retro fabric for body

Striped fabric (preferably red and white)

Teal, red, and yellow felt

3 plastic eyes

Iron

2 novelty buttons

Lace trim

FINISHED PROJECT SIZE AS PICTURED IS 5 X 13 INCHES (BODY ONLY). ARMS AND LEGS ARE 5 INCHES LONG.

How to Create Polly

1 Using the photograph as a guide, draw or trace, and then enlarge and cut out the pattern pieces. Pin the body, eye, leg, and arm pieces to the appropriate fabric, and cut out two of each.

2 Cut out and sew on the felt lips and eyes. Attach a plastic eyeball to the middle of each yellow felt circle.

3 With right sides together, sew together the eyes, arms, and legs, leaving the bottom of each piece open. Turn each piece right side out.

4 It's time to stuff. Tightly stuff the arms and legs. The stuffing in the eyes should be loose. These pieces will be sewn into the main body, so leave about a 3/4 to 1-inch area at the opening of each unstuffed.

5 Iron a 1/2-inch hem at the top and bottom of the body parts. Lay the front body piece so that it overlaps the front head piece by

about 1/2 inch. Sew the body to the head using a decorative stitch. Repeat with the back head and body pieces.

6 Use a decorative stitch to sew on the teal felt rectangle. Sew on the novelty buttons.

7 Place the front body piece faceup and lay the eyes and arms in position, facing inward. Make sure the ends overlap the seam enough to get sewn in securely. Place the back body piece on top, with the right side facing down. Pin and sew from one bottom edge of Polly's body all the way around to the other bottom edge, leaving the straight edge open for stuffing.

8 Turn Polly's body right side out and stuff it until firm. Fold under the bottom edges of the body fabric, creating a 1/2-inch hem. Place the top 1 inch of the legs inside the body, and pin to secure. Stitch the opening closed, and sew on lace trim.

DESIGNER: **BECK WHEELER**

Polly

31

Gingerbread Men

The ones that got away. These little fellas were lucky enough to escape the fate of many of their friends. Unfortunately they didn't go completely unharmed, but at least they survived to tell the tale.

Stuff You'll Need

Tailor's chalk

2 pieces of felt (as close to the color of gingerbread as possible)

White embroidery thread

2 black buttons

2 white buttons

Red embroidery thread

FINISHED PROJECT SIZE AS PICTURED IS 5 1/2 X 7 3/4 INCHES.

DESIGNER: **KATE SUTTON**

How to Create a Gingerbread Man

1 Using the photograph as a guide, draw or trace, and then enlarge and cut out the pattern pieces. Pin the pattern to the felt, trace around with tailor's chalk, and cut out two pieces. Pin the two pieces together with the rights sides of the fabric facing each other.

2 Decide where you would like to position your "bite," and cut off that section of the gingerbread man.

3 Machine or hand-sew the pieces together, leaving a 1/8-inch seam allowance. Leave a 2-inch gap to allow you to turn it right side out.

4 Turn the gingerbread man right side out, and stuff him with the polyester fiber, packing it quite tight. Hand-stitch the opening closed.

5 To create the "icing," use the white embroidery thread to make running stitches all around the gingerbread man. Sew the buttons into place. Sew the mouth with red embroidery thread using a backstitch.

A typical Aussie, Loud Pants Pup likes nothing more than lazing around in his Loud pants, barbecue fork in one hand, and a fly swat in the other. Just don't mention the word hot dog, and he'll be your best mate.

Stuff You'll Need

2 pieces of purple felt (for body)

Your favorite loud cotton fabric (for pants)

Striped cotton fabric (for legs)

Light brown felt

Embroidery floss

FINISHED PROJECT SIZE AS PICTURED IS 5 X 11 INCHES.

34

How to Create Loud Pants Pup

1 Using the photograph as a guide, draw or trace, and then enlarge and cut out the pattern pieces.

2 Pin the four corners of the two purple felt pieces together. Make sure the material is a few inches larger in size than your pattern. This will be Loud Pant's body form. Trace the pattern onto the felt using tailor's chalk.

3 Re-pin the felt just inside the traced shape. Trim around the pattern, leaving an approximate 1/4-inch seam allowance.

4 Repeat steps 2 and 3 for the pants and legs.

5 Cut out felt circles for Pup's eye patches and nose and sew them on. Embroider Pup's mouth and an "X" in each eye.

6 With right sides together, sew the pants to the felt body. Repeat for the other side of the body.

7 Sew the front and back of each striped leg together, leaving the top open. Stuff and sew closed.

8 Place the front body piece faceup and lay the legs in position, facing inward. Pin their tops to the bottom edge of the pants. Lay the back body piece on top, with the right side facing down. Sew around the outside of the body leaving the straight edge under one of Pup's arms open for stuffing.

9 Trim away any excess felt around the sewn body form, and snip into any tight corners to prevent bunching. Turn the body form right side out.

10 Stuff the body beginning at the bottom and working your way up. Be careful not to stuff too hard or the seams may split. Hand-stitch closed.

DESIGNER: **CARLY SCHWERDT**

Loud
Pants
Pup

Hexapus

Heloise is a hexapus who used to be an administrative assistant to a monopus, who couldn't type. She left that career to pursue professional ice skating. These days, crowds numbering in the millions swarm to watch her spin and twirl. Her triple axle is truly mind-boggling.

Stuff You'll Need

Heloise hexapus template
  (see page 112)

Tailor's chalk

Fabric scraps in assorted colors and textures (one color for body, one for legs, contrasting color for eye patch)*

6 flexible hair rollers, 10-inches long, with 1/2-inch diameter

Upholstery thread and needle

Lentils or poly beads

2 fabric-covered buttons about 3/4-inch diameter

2 small buttons (for eyes) of varying sizes

Embroidery floss (for details)

*Note: Suggested fabrics are any type that has texture and won't fray, including upholstery velvet and felted wool.

FINISHED PROJECT SIZE AS PICTURED HAS
A 4 X 2 1/2-INCH BODY.

How to Create Heloise

1 Enlarge, copy, and cut out the pattern pieces. Using tailor's chalk, trace six body pieces and six leg pieces onto your selected fabrics, and cut them out.

2 Leave a 1/4-inch seam allowance, and with right sides together, sew two body pieces from point A to B (refer to template) on one side only, so you can still open the sewn piece. Add another body piece. Back-tack to secure firmly at each point. Repeat the process, except this time sew from point C to D.

3 Repeat step 2 with the remaining three body pieces.

4 Now you have two body halves. Carefully match the point A's, and pin them together with the right sides facing each other. Sew them together from point B to A, then on to the other point B. Make a small but secure tack at point C on each side. Don't sew from C to D.

5 Fold each leg piece in half lengthwise, right sides facing, and sew with a 1/4-inch seam allowance, leaving the straight end open. Trim leg seam allowances to 1/8 inch. Notch the seam allowances on the body pieces. Turn the body and legs right side out.

6 Firmly stuff the body with polyester fiber until you reach the leg openings. Slide one flexible hair roller through each leg opening so that they all meet in the center of the body. With upholstery thread, securely tie the ends of the rollers together inside the body.

7 Fill the rest of the body area up with lentils or polyester beads. Stuff as firmly

DESIGNER: **JESSICA CROKER**

as you possibly can, making sure to get in between and around the hair rollers. Use a ladder stitch to sew the body closed.

8 Stuff the rounded foot end of each leg with a cotton ball-sized piece of stuffing. Slide each leg piece over a hair roller. Turn the open edge down 1/8 to 1/4 inch. Make sure the leg seam is facing down and matches up with the seam on the bottom of the body. Use a ladder stitch to secure legs to the body.

9 To tuft the body, take a length of upholstery thread and attach it to one covered button. Send your needle down through the top of the body where all the pattern pieces meet, and then out the bottom where all of the pattern pieces meet. Thread on your second covered button and push your needle back to the top. Go through the buttons in this manner a couple of times, and pull the thread tight until your body is squished the way you like it. Tie securely and trim your thread.

10 Cut your eye patch from a contrasting color of fabric. Use straight pins through the holes of each eye button to experiment with eye placement on your little guy. Blanket-stitch the patch in place, sew on the eye buttons, embroider the mouth—and don't forget the eyebrows!!

Harry

All the girls swoon over Harry and his impressive woolly chest, but none have captured his heart. To find out why, turn to page 104. But be forewarned, Harry's lifestyle is not for the prudish.

Stuff You'll Need

Felt

Tailor's chalk

Beanie or polypropylene pellets

Craft glue

Black embroidery floss

Large-eyed needle

FINISHED PROJECT SIZE AS PICTURED IS 7 X 10 INCHES.

How to Create Harry

1 Using the photograph as a guide, draw or trace, and then enlarge and cut out the pattern pieces.

2 Pin the four corners of two pieces of felt together. Make sure the material is a few inches larger in size than your pattern. This will become Harry's body form. Trace around the pattern with tailor's chalk.

3 Re-pin felt just inside of the traced shape. Remove corner pins. Trim around the pattern, leaving approximately 1/4-inch allowance.

4 Sew around the outline of the body form, leaving a 2-inch opening at the side of Harry's head for turning and stuffing.

5 Trim away any excess felt around the sewn body form, and then turn it right side out.

6 Stuff the body form, alternating between a mixture of pellets and polyester stuffing. Stuff Harry at the bottom first, then gradually fill towards the top.

7 Hand-stitch the body form closed.

8 Make Harry's eyes and mouth out of felt. Attach the felt details with crafter's glue.

9 Use black embroidery floss for Harry's chest hair. Thread an uncut length of the floss through the eye of a larger-sized needle. Carefully insert the threaded needle into the far left side of Harry's chest, doing so in two areas that are in line with one another (figure 1). Pull out about four to five inches of floss from both the top and the bottom areas. Cut the floss so the long end remains threaded in the needle. That way, you won't need to rethread the needle

FIGURE 1

DESIGNER: **GRACE MONTEMAR**

each time you finish adding a tuft of Harry's chest hair. Tie a knot flush against Harry's chest in both of the floss pieces. Trim the floss to your desired length. Try to stagger the lengths so they're not too perfect, so they mimic actual chest hair. It also helps to cut them at angles.

10 Repeat this process, working from the left to the right side of Harry's chest until the hair appears "full" and scraggly. Stagger the hair tufts from top to bottom.

Variations

Harry has a group of close-knit friends based on mutual respect and not appearances. While their body forms may be simple, their personalities are complex.

Catzilla

Catzilla is the unfortunate by-product of an unholy love triangle amongst a cat, a sweater, and an iguana. He likes pillaging, belly rubs, and smiting wool moths with his fierce tuna breath. He dislikes rain, car rides, and onions.

Stuff You'll Need

Catzilla template (see page 113)

Scraps of felt or wool

Old wool sweater (see Creating Felted Wool Fabric on page 9)

FINISHED PROJECT SIZE AS PICTURED IS 8¹/₂ X 9 INCHES.

How to Create Catzilla

1 Enlarge, copy, and cut out the pattern pieces. Using the pattern as your guide, cut out all facial embellishments, footpads, and spikes from felt.

2 Cut out two squares from the body of your sweater, and place them right sides together.

3 Place the body pattern on top of your squares, and pin through the pattern and both squares to keep everything in place.

4 Carefully machine-stitch just along the outside edge of the pattern. Stitch around all edges of the body except for the gap between the legs. Leave this area open for turning the material and for stuffing.

5 Now that everything is sewn together, unpin the pattern from the squares, and carefully cut around the body, taking care to leave roughly a ¹/₄-inch seam allowance on all sides.

Turn right side out, and stuff firmly. Use small, tight, whipstitches to hand-sew the leg opening closed.

6 Using the tail pattern, cut out a tail from a piece of sweater. Fold it in half lengthwise, right sides together, aligning the long edges. Whipstitch those edges closed. Turn right side out and hand-stitch the spikes on along the seam. Stuff firmly. Hand-stitch to the backside of the body, about 1 inch

above the leg opening to enable the tail to act as a tripod. Then Catzilla can stand on his own.

7 Hand-stitch Catzilla's facial features with coordinating thread. Add a couple more spikes to the back, and stitch footpads to the bottoms of the feet. Catzilla is now ready to inflict terror upon the moths of the world.

DESIGNER: **BERTHA CROWLEY**

Felix Von Schnapps

Felix Von Schnapps has no need for arms. His attendants serve him night and day, meeting his every need. He's a fashionable fellow—his dapper suits are hand-tailored by an exclusive London haberdashery. Never call on Felix on a Monday afternoon—that's when he's busy tasting cheese.

Stuff You'll Need

White cotton fabric

Blue faux fur

Orange felt

Suiting material (wool or wool blend)

Green felt

Striped cotton fabric

Fabric marker or colorfast ink

Iron

2 different-sized buttons

2 plastic claws

FINISHED PROJECT SIZE AS PICTURED IS 12 X 17 INCHES.

How to Create Felix Von Schnapps

1 Using the photograph as a guide, draw or trace, and then enlarge and cut out the pattern pieces. Pin the pattern pieces to the appropriate fabric, and cut out two of each.

2 Using the fabric marker or fabric inks, draw Felix's face onto one of the white head pieces.

3 Fold over and iron both the top edges of the body pieces to create a 1/2-inch hem. Overlap the top edge of the body piece over the head piece, and sew together using a decorative stitch with bright, contrasting-colored thread. Repeat with the back head and body pieces.

4 Stitch the green felt rectangle onto his front. Sew the two buttons in place.

5 Place two leg fabric pieces with right sides together. Position a claw so it points inwards, with at least 1/4 inch of the claw base outside of the seam line. Sew the leg together, leaving the top open. Turn right side out and stuff. Repeat for the other leg.

6 Sew the ears together, leaving the base edge open, and then turn them right side out. Fold the bottom edge of each ear inward, and tack.

7 Place the front body piece facedown, and lay the ears in position, facing inward. Make sure they overlap enough to get sewn into the seams. Place the back body piece on top, with the right side facing down. Pin and sew from one bottom edge of Felix's body all the way around to the other bottom edge, leaving the straight edge open for stuffing.

8 Turn Felix's body right side out, and stuff it until firm. Fold under the bottom edge of the body fabric, creating a 1/2-inch hem. Place the top 1 inch of the legs inside the body, and pin to secure. Sew the opening closed.

DESIGNER: **BECK WHEELER**

Plucky

Don't mess with the rooster. That's right, what Plucky lacks in size he makes up for in attitude. Some call it confidence, and some call it a Napoleon complex. We call it Plucky Power.

Stuff You'll Need

Plucky template (see page 114)

Yellow and red polar fleece

Orange, yellow, and white felt

Yard of double-sided fusible fabric web

Iron

2 black buttons, one larger than the other

2 white buttons, one larger than the other, sized to fit inside the black buttons

Orange and white thread

FINISHED PROJECT SIZE AS PICTURED IS 11 X 11 INCHES.

How to Create Plucky

1 Enlarge, copy, and cut out the pattern pieces. On the wrong side of the yellow fleece, pin the front body pattern to the fabric, following the pattern grain lines. Cut out one front body piece. Mark the notches with the pencil. Flip the piece so the right side is facing up, and place the pattern piece back on it. Mark the position of the eyes and beak.

2 To cut the two back body pieces, fold another piece of yellow fleece in half on the grain. Pin the back body pattern piece to the folded fabric, and cut out.

3 Fold the red polar fleece in half on the grain and pin the top head pattern piece down. Cut out and mark the notches.

4 Cut out rectangles from the felt pieces for the beak, teeth, wings, and feet.

5 Set your iron on "steam." Iron a rectangle of double-sided fusible fabric web, rough side up, to the orange felt. Do not peel off the paper backing yet. Set aside. Iron a small rectangle of double-sided fusible fabric web to a yellow felt rectangle. After it cools, peel off the paper backing. Iron the other piece of yellow felt to the glue side of the first piece of felt. Do the same for the white felt pieces.

6 Pin the beak pattern to the orange felt, and cut out one. Pin the wings and feet patterns on the yellow felt, and cut two of each. To make the teeth, cut a rectangular piece of white felt. Cut teeth in evenly spaced intervals perpendicular to the length, leaving 1/8 inch uncut at the top edge.

7 Remove the paper backing from the beak. Center the teeth on the beak and pin them down in a curved shape.

Zigzag stitch over the 1/8-inch top edge of the teeth. Center the beak on the marks on the right side of the front body, secure with pins, and zigzag stitch around the edge. Sew on the buttons using the orange thread.

8 Topstitch the wings and feet 1/8 inch from the edge with orange thread.

9 Flip the back body pieces so that the wrong sides face each other. This is how you get the raw edge for the back seam. Pin the center back seam together, and stitch with a 1/4-inch seam allowance.

10 Pin the front body top edge to the front head bottom edge, right sides facing each other, and sew with a 1/4-inch seam allowance. Do the same for the back body and back head.

11 Baste the wings and feet into position as marked with the notches on the wrong side of the front body piece.

12 Sew the front and back together. Using the notches to line up the pieces, pin the front and back bodies together with right sides facing each other. Sew all around with a 1/4-inch seam allowance. Turn Plucky inside out.

13 Start stuffing Plucky by filling in the head with small clumps of stuffing and working your way down, stuffing the body with handful-sized stuffing clumps until he is full. Hand-sew the opening to close the shape.

DESIGNER: **RACHEL CHOW** AND **JASON CARPENTER**

Pig/Duck

The Pig/Duck is a contented migratory swine-type animal that likes to roll in mud. As this is detrimental to the sheen of its feathers, Pig/Duck only rolls in mud when it's time to molt. Endowed with both wings and hooves, the Pig/Duck is an avid tap dancer. You can often hear it tapping, flapping, and singing its merry "quoink" on sunny days.

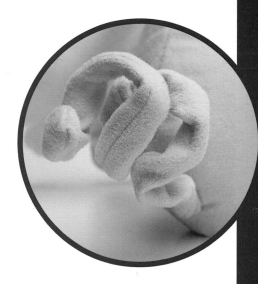

Stuff You'll Need

Pig/Duck template (see page 115)

Yellow plush

Pink plush

2 small black buttons (for eyes)

Embroidery needle

Black embroidery floss

Batting

Pipe cleaner or any other wire
(for tail)

FINISHED PROJECT SIZE AS PICTURED IS 11½ X 8 INCHES FOR THE BODY, AND 2½ X 5 INCHES FOR EACH LEG.

How to Create a Pig/Duck

1 Enlarge, copy, and cut out the pattern pieces. Pin the patterns on your fabric, right sides up. Cut the body pieces first, adding an ⅛-inch to ¼-inch seam allowance. Repeat with each individual leg.

2 Place the two pieces of the main body right sides together, and sew from the tail area to the neck, leaving a big opening in the belly area for where you add the legs. Turn right side out and set aside.

3 Sew one side of the leg to its hoof, then sew the back side of the leg to the other side of the hoof. Put the right sides of those two pieces together, and sew around the leg on the wrong side of the fabric, leaving the top of the leg open. Turn right-side out and stuff. Repeat this procedure with the other three legs.

4 Sew button eyes to the head. Embroider the nostril holes on the front piece of the beak, and sew the right sides together, leaving a small opening at one end of the beak for stuffing. Turn right side out, stuff, and then sew the opening closed.

5 Stuff the body cavity, and then pin and hand-sew the belly closed. Pin each leg in position, and attach them with a ladder stitch. Pin the beak in place, and hand-stitch around it, securing it to the face.

6 To make the wings, cut out a piece of batting that is slightly smaller in size than the wing pattern. Place right sides of the material together, lay the batting on top, and sew all the way around except for the straight edge. Turn right side out. Sew the edge closed, and attach to the body using the photo as a guide for placement.

7 Sew the tail pieces together and turn right side out. Bend the tip of a pipe cleaner or wire into a loop so it does not poke through the fabric. Wrap stuffing around the wire and insert in the tail. Sew the tail closed and stitch it in place. Wrap the tail around a pencil to make it curl.

49

DESIGNER: **LIZETTE GRECO**

Candy Apple Neko

Candy Apple Neko is the tasty treat of Tokyo, and is as zany as her candy cane-striped obi. She takes the train every day to work at Kooki's Candy Shoppe, where she loves her job and will forever stay plump working there.

Stuff You'll Need

Candy Apple Neko template
(see page 116)

Red faux fur

Cherry-red felt

Yellow felt

Green faux fur

Candy cane-striped fabric

Fabric for scarf

FINISHED PROJECT SIZE AS PICTURED IS 6¹/₂ X 6¹/₂ INCHES.

How to Create a Candy Apple Neko

1 Enlarge, copy, and cut out the pattern pieces. Pin the pieces to the appropriate material and cut out. For the obi, cut a strip of fabric that will wrap around your Neko's "waist".

2 Fold the red faux fur in half and cut a half-moon for each cheek, and a half-heart of red felt for the nose. To make the face, center the small face piece on top of the larger head piece. Pin them together at the top and bottom to keep them in place.

3 Using the photo as a guide for placement, stitch the eyes, lashes, whiskers, and mouth onto the face using the black thread. Attach the felt heart nose and the cheek fuzzies with an "X" in the middle of each.

4 Hand-sew a straight stitch around the head, about ¹/₈ inch from the edge of the material. Leave a small opening to insert stuffing. Push small bits of polyester fiber inside until the head is puffed and firm. Be careful not to overstuff, or the seams will stretch. Finish stitching the head closed.

5 For your final stitch, bring the needle out through the side of the head, in between the front and back fabric pieces.

6 Pin the yellow and red ear pieces to the head. Hand-stitch the joined pieces to the top right of the head, across the lip of the fabric. Repeat with the left red ear.

7 Sew your heart piece onto the body piece. Pin the two body pieces together at the top and bottom, and then sew around the perimeter about ¹/₈ inch from the edge, leaving a hole for stuffing. Stuff your body until it's firm, and then sew it shut.

8 Now it's time to sew the head to the body. Use a few pins to hold the head on the body. Place the lower lip of the head in front of the upper lip of the body, and sew the two pieces together. Wrap the scarf around the neck and tie the ends together.

DESIGNER: **ASHLEY BAKER**

9 Wrap the obi around the center of the tummy, pin it in the back, and do a few whipstitches to hold it in place.

10 Turn your Neko so its chest is lying on the ground and sew one end of the tail to the back of the Neko's fuzzy rear end. Twist the tail around a few times, then attach it to the side of the chest with a single stitch, about an inch above the obi. Add a final stitch near the tip of the tail on the side of the head.

11 Whipstitch the smooth edges of the wings in place on the back, using the photo as a guide for placement.

Variations

One can never have enough Nekos— honestly, the more, the better. Whether making a pastel Neko, a retro Neko, or an incredibly bright Neko, picking out the fabric is half the fun. Let the pattern of the material inspire you to try variations on the basic Neko form, like the "cat-fish" pictured here (note the "scale" pattern).

Monsieur Octopus

Monsieur Octopus lives off the coast of France. He spends most of his time trying to get the attention of Maria, a hot lady octopus; unfortunately, she is not interested. He likes baking cakes, cycling, and collecting shells.

Stuff You'll Need

Bright material for the body

8 old ties

Tailor's chalk

2 different-sized buttons
   (for the eyes)

FINISHED PROJECT SIZE AS PICTURED HAS A 9 X 7¹⁄₄-INCH BODY WITH 6¹⁄₄-INCH TENTACLES.

How to Create Monsieur Octopus

1 Using the photograph as a guide, draw or trace, and then enlarge and cut out the body pattern piece. Cut out two main body pieces from your chosen fabric.

2 Cut the narrow end off a tie so it is about 9 inches long. Stuff the tie with a little polyester fiber. Stitch along the seam, fold over the end of the tie, and sew closed (figure 1).

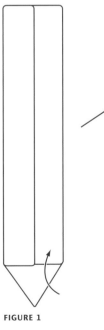

FIGURE 1

DESIGNER: **KATE SUTTON**

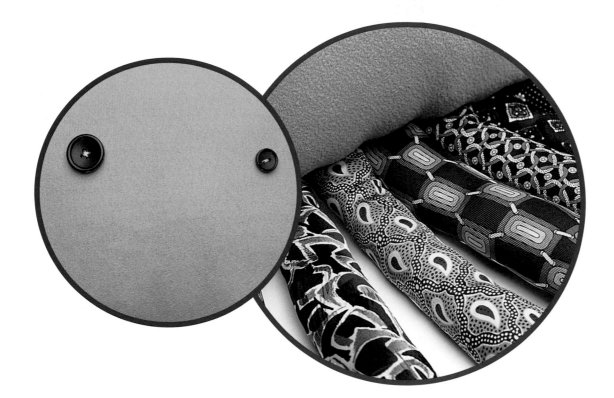

3 Place the legs along the right side of the fabric of one of the body pieces (figure 2). Place the other body piece over the first to form a sandwich, with the legs in the middle. Make sure the right sides are facing each other, and tack around the edge of the main body (figure 3).

4 Sew all around the edge, leaving a 2-inch gap to allow you to turn it right side out.

5 Turn right side out, stuff, and then hand-stitch the opening closed. Sew the buttons on for the eyes.

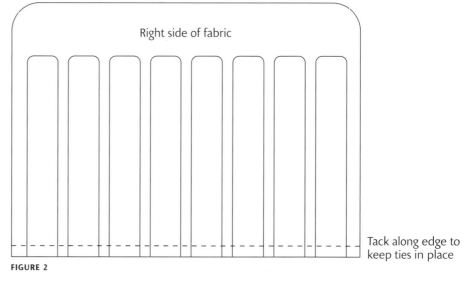

Right side of fabric

Tack along edge to keep ties in place

FIGURE 2

FIGURE 3

Apple Tree

*Take him home and you're bound to become a real tree hugger!
That's not a squirrel hiding inside his trunk; that's the tree
spirit himself.*

Stuff You'll Need

- **Apple Tree template** (see page 117)
- **Shaggy green fur**
- **Textured, brown fabric**
- **Black felt scrap**
- **White felt scrap** (optional)
- **2 plastic eyes and washers**
- **9 red pom-poms**, 1½ or 2 inches in diameter
- **Hot glue and glue gun**

FINISHED PROJECT SIZE AS PICTURED IS 8 X 12 INCHES.

How to Create Apple Tree

1 Enlarge, copy, and cut out the pattern pieces. Cut out four treetop pieces from the green fur. Brush the long fur away from the edges and pin two of the pieces together, with the furry sides facing each other.

2 Stitch along one side from top to bottom. Repeat with the other two treetop pieces.

3 Unfold each half and place them flat against each other, fuzzy sides together. Pin and stitch all the way around, leaving the short, straight edge open.

4 Cut three trunk pieces and one bottom piece from brown fabric. Anything with a texture will work well as bark. The trunk in the photo was an old, rust-colored, nubbly-textured curtain.

5 Pin two trunk pieces together, right sides facing each other, and sew along one side edge. Sew the third trunk piece on in the same way, and then sew the first and third pieces together to form the circumference of the trunk.

6 Pin the tree bottom to the trunk, aligning the three points of the triangle to the three points of the bottom of the trunk. Again, make sure the right sides are facing each other. Stitch all the way around the triangle. Turn the trunk right side out using a long, blunt object inside to help poke out the points at the bottom of the trunk.

7 Cut out the eye area from a small piece of black felt. If the eyes you have chosen are transparent like the yellow ones pictured, cut out a small circle of white felt, and then cut a little hole in the middle. Place this on the shaft of the eye, and it will make the color stand out better on top of the black felt. Disregard this step if your eyes are opaque.

8 Using the eye area pattern piece as a guide, mark two dots on the trunk where the eyeholes will go. Align the pattern over one of the seams of the trunk and hold flat while marking through the little holes. Snip a tiny hole in each place that you just marked for the eyes. Place each eye through the black felt and then the trunk. Secure in place on the inside with a washer.

9 Place the trunk inside the still inside-out treetop. Pin the treetop to the trunk and stitch around, leaving about a 1½-inch opening. Be sure to backstitch at the beginning and end of the seam for strength. Turn inside out and stuff with polyester fiber, and then hand-stitch the opening closed.

10 Before applying each apple (pom-pom), spread out the shaggy fur at the spot where you want to place it. Then put some hot glue on a pom-pom and hold it in place for about one minute.

DESIGNER: **JENNY HARADA**

Gremlins

These two are handy monsters to have around. When not repairing computers, they spend their free time watching home improvement programs, and take great delight in hanging sheetrock and replacing faucets. Just be prepared to have your home's walls moved on a daily basis.

Stuff You'll Need

Gremlin template (see page 118)

Tailor's chalk

Fabric of your choice

Tiny scrap of felt (preferably wool) for teeth

Lentils or polypropylene pellets

Yarn for hair

2 little black beads (for eyes)

Embroidery floss (for eyebrows)

FINISHED PROJECT SIZE AS PICTURED IS 3¹/₂ X 5 INCHES FOR THE BODY. THE ARMS ARE AN ADDITIONAL 3 INCHES LONG, AND THE LEGS ARE 3¹/₂ INCHES LONG.

DESIGNER: **JESSICA CROKER**

How to Create a Gremlin

1 Enlarge, copy, and cut out the pattern pieces. Using tailor's chalk, trace and then cut out the pieces from the fabric of your choice. Trace and cut out the teeth from felt.

2 Pin two arm pieces together and sew with a ¹/₄-inch seam allowance, right sides facing, leaving the straight edge open. Sew the remaining arm and leg pieces likewise. Notch seam allowances on the curves, and turn the arms and legs right side out.

3 Stuff each arm and leg with a tablespoon or two of lentils or polypropylene pellets. Don't overstuff— you want them to remain floppy. Set them all to the side.

4 Lay one body piece right side up in front of you. Between points A and B, loop your yarn up and down, lining up the tops of the loops with the edge of the fabric. Baste the yarn in place about ¹/₄ inch or less from the edge.

5 with the right side of the fabric facing up, place the front body piece on your work surface. Pin the open end of one arm to the edge of the body piece, between points C and D (marked on the template). Make sure the arm faces inward. Baste in place ¹/₄ inch or less from the edge. Repeat with the other arm between points E and F.

6 Fold the top of one leg so that the front and back seams meet. Similar to what you did with the arms, pin the open edge of the leg to the body piece, between points G and H. Make sure the toe end of the foot is facing down toward the right side of the body fabric. Baste in place 1/4 inch or less from the edge. Repeat with the other leg between points I and J.

7 Pin and then sew one side of the bottom gusset, right side down, across the bottom of the body piece, sandwiching the basted leg edges between the body fabric and the bottom gusset fabric. Use a 1/2-inch seam allowance.

8 Place and pin the back body piece, right side down, over the body piece with limbs and hair attached. Sew the sides and top of the body pieces together with a 1/2-inch seam allowance. Sew the bottom edge of the back body piece halfway across the remaining edge of the bottom gusset, leaving an opening for turning.

9 Cut notches in the seam allowance at the corners. Turn your gremlin right side out.

10 Stuff the top of the head with a handful of polyester fiber, then about 1/2 cup of lentils or pellets. Fold the seam allowance in and sew the opening shut.

11 To make an ear, pinch across one top corner so that the top and side seams line up with each other. Tack with one stitch close to the hair. Sew on the teeth along the top edge only. Sew on the eyes and embroider eyebrows.

Batty Cat Bubbles

Batty Cat Bubbles is currently mired in an identity crisis. Is he a cat? Is he a bat? With a tail like his, he could even be a dragon! Whatever he is, one thing is for sure—he is definitely a sweetheart...just look at that face.

Stuff You'll Need

Batty Cat Bubbles template (see page 119)

Tracing paper

Old suit material

Scrap pieces of wool felt (for nose, cheeks, eyes, teeth, and wings)

Sewing machine and thread (in black, coral, and a contrasting color to the suit material)

Pinking shears

Needle-nose pliers

8 inches of 16-gauge wire

FINISHED PROJECT SIZE AS PICTURED IS 4¹/₂ X 7¹/₂ INCHES.

How to Create Batty Cat Bubbles

1 Enlarge and copy the pattern pieces. Trace the pattern onto tracing paper. Pin the tracing paper to the top of the right side of a suit material, and sew a basting stitch ¹/₈ inch outside of the pattern line through the tracing paper to make the seam lines.

2 Cut out the wings, eyes, nose, cheeks, and teeth from respective wool felt colors.

3 Starting with the nose, pin the felt feature pieces onto the torso. Sew along the edge of the piece two or three passes using black thread. Follow with the whites of the eyes, the irises, cheeks, and teeth.

4 To sew the mouth, sew along the mouth line, making two or three passes with black thread. Make another two or three passes with coral thread.

5 With right sides together, sew the arms along the seam lines. Trim the seams to ¹/₄ inch with pinking shears. Clip diagonal notches at the corners. Turn the arms right side out, and stuff.

6 Using a basting stitch, sew a ⁵/₈-inch seam along the arm openings. Pin the arms to the face panel side of Batty Cat, with the tops of the arms even with the mouth line, and with the "fingers" facing inward, toward his belly. Sew a ¹/₄-inch seam along each arm opening.

7 Place the face panel on top of the back panel, so the right sides are together. Sew a seam ¹/₈ inch INSIDE the basting stitch, leaving a 2-inch opening under one of the arms for

62

DESIGNER: **AMY PROFF LYONS**

turning right side out. Use the pinking shears to trim the seams to $1/4$ inch. Clip diagonal notches at corners.

8 Turn the torso right side out and stuff. Use a ladder stitch to close the opening under the arm.

9 To make the tail, fold a piece of suit material in half to form a rectangle. Starting $1/2$ inch from the fold, sew down the length of the rectangle, tapering off toward the fold at the end of the fabric piece. Trim away any excess fabric with pinking shears.

10 Using needle-nose pliers, bend one end of the wire into a small circle and insert it into the tail piece. Shape the wire into a U-shape, and position it on Batty Cat's bum so that it will function as a stand. Pin in place, then attach with a tack stitch.

11 Pin the felt wings in place on Batty Cat's back. Attach with a tack stitch at the top and side points.

Dibley

Dibley is too hard on himself. He views his major disappointments in life as coming in second place in the regional pole vaulting championship, reading only the Cliff's Notes of Catcher in the Rye, *and having a cavity. You can probably find him kicking himself over some spilled milk.*

Stuff You'll Need

Fleece for body

Felt for mouth and ears

Embroidery needle

Black embroidery floss for eyes
(size 25 doubled on your needle
is ideal)

Felt for teeth

FINISHED PROJECT SIZE AS PICTURED IS 9¹/₂ X 7¹/₂ INCHES.

How to Create a Dibley Blobby

1 Using the photograph as a guide, draw or trace, and then enlarge and cut out the pattern pieces.

2 Fold the fleece fabric in half, pin the body pattern to the fabric, and cut it out. Now you should have two body pieces.

3 Use the mouth pattern and cut one piece out of felt. Cut out two ears using the patterns.

4 Lay one of the fleece body pieces down right side up. Pin the felt pieces on the body. Leave seam allowances around exterior edges, and stitch the felt pieces onto the single-layer body. After stitching, pull your threads to the backside with a needle, knot them, and snip. This leaves a clean front.

5 Use embroidery floss to stitch on the eyes. To make Dibley's teeth, fold the felt in half, stitch two teeth onto the folded felt, THEN cut out (see page 72).

6 Now you are ready to put Dibley together. Place the back body piece right side up. Place the two felt teeth on the fleece with the rough edges along the seam edge. Place the front body piece right side down on top, sandwiching the teeth. Pin the pieces together, making sure to catch the teeth in the pins. Stitch along the edge with a ³/₈-inch seam. Make sure not to catch the felt mouth and the ears in the seam, but making sure to catch the felt teeth in the seam. Leave approximately a 2-inch gap unsewn along the back side for turning your Blobby right side out and for stuffing. Back-tack the start and end of the stitching.

7 Trim and clip the seams close to the stitching on the curves, corners, and between the toes and ears. Be careful not to clip any seams! Turn Dibley inside out.

8 Stuff with polyester fiber. Hand-sew the stuffing hole closed. Stitch in the ditch to hide your stitching.

DESIGNER: **MARIA SAMUELSON**

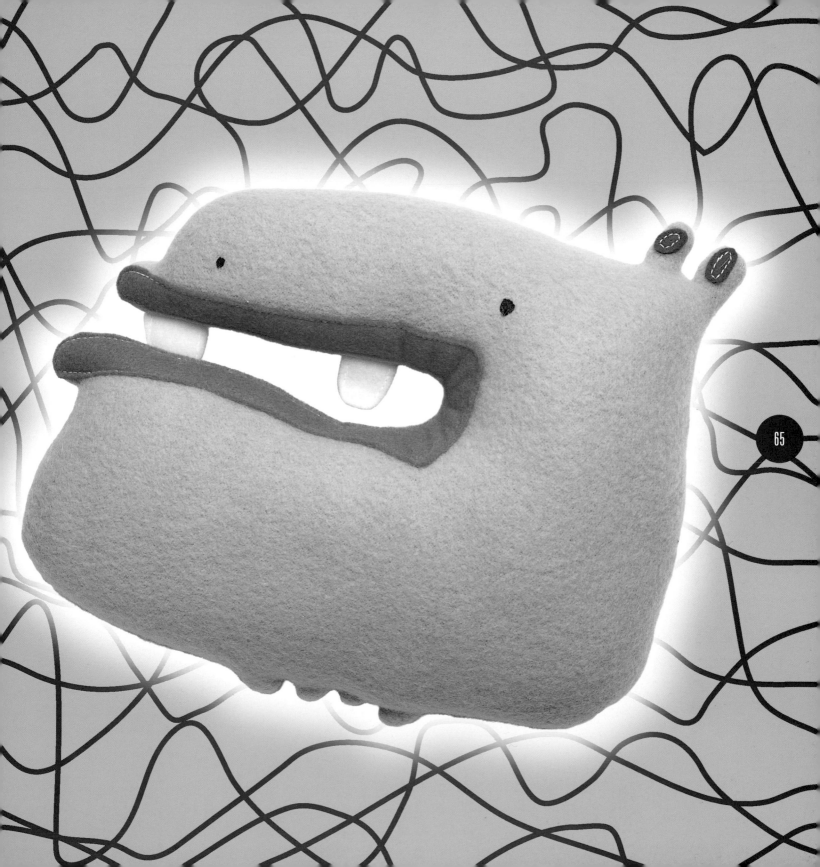

Llorie
the Bipolar Cloud

Llorie spends her days watching over the world's ups and downs. She can't help but puff and glow for every budding flower, but she also bawls her eyes out when any blade of grass is cut. Being a bipolar cloud is a rough gig, but Llorie's friend Tinkle, the Not-So-Bright Star, is always helping her look for her silver lining. Be careful when approaching the pair, though—Tinkle's jealous robot boyfriend, Crush, can be counted on to kill you with kindness, or with a swift swat to the trachea. (See the pair pictured on page 69.)

Stuff You'll Need

- Happy fabric* (white and fluffy)
- Sad fabric* (gray and gloomy)
- Colored pencil or tailor's chalk
- Craft knife or rotary cutter
- Self-healing cutting mat or piece of thick cardboard
- White contrasting fabric* (for tooth and tear)
- Embroidery needle
- Black and white embroidery floss

*Tip: Choosing fabrics that won't ravel makes all the curvy cuts a lot easier. Synthetic furs, polar fleece, or felts are great. If you go with felt, make sure there is some wool in it—it is SO much easier to work with than the all-polyester stuff.

FINISHED PROJECT SIZE AS PICTURED IS 12 1/2 X 7 INCHES (BODY ONLY).

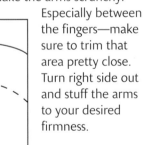

FIGURE 1

How to Create LLorie

1 Using the photograph as a guide, draw or trace, and then enlarge and cut out the pattern pieces. Face the right sides (or fuzzy sides) of the happy and sad fabrics together. Pin the arm pattern to the fabric, leaving at least 1/2 inch outside of the pattern so you will have something to stitch into. Trace the pattern with your pencil or chalk. Flip the pattern over and trace it again in another spot, making a new arm that is a mirror-image of the first one. Keep the pins in the arms and cut each one out, so you end up with one left arm and one right arm, each happy on one side, sad on the other.

2 Sew each arm together, leaving the "shoulder" open for turning and stuffing. In the points between the fingers, make sure to do a couple of squared-off stitches—this will help the fabric lay flatter when you invert the arms (figure 1). After sewing them together, trim off any bulk outside your stitching that might make the arms scrunchy. Especially between the fingers—make sure to trim that area pretty close. Turn right side out and stuff the arms to your desired firmness.

3 Face the right sides of the happy and sad fabrics together again. Pin the body pattern to the fabric, leaving at least 1/2 inch outside the pattern. Trace the shape onto the fabric, marking the place where the arms will attach. And be sure to put the smile on the happy side!

4 Cut out the outside of the fabric, again leaving at least 1/2-inch of fabric to sew together. Use your craft knife or rotary cutter to cut the through-and-through mouth out of the center of both fabric pieces. Use a self-healing cutting mat or a piece of cardboard to protect your work surface.

5 Now for the fun part: take apart your fabric sandwich and place the arms inside, lining them up to the marks you made previously. Be sure to make them point up for the happy side and down for the sad side (figure 2). Pin the arms into place first, and then continue pinning around the rest of the shape, lining up each poof of the cloud. There's no need to leave any openings on the outside edge, but leave the mouth open for now.

6 Now sew all the way around the entire edge. Reach in through the open mouth, and grab an arm. Invert your cloud and give it a hug. Hand-sew the flat side of the mouth. You can use a hidden stitch if your fabric isn't fuzzy enough to hide the stitches, but a whipstitch works great, too.

7 Through the part of the mouth that is still open, stuff the cloud behind the hand-stitching you just put in—while you can still reach it.

DESIGNER: **DAVID HUYCK**

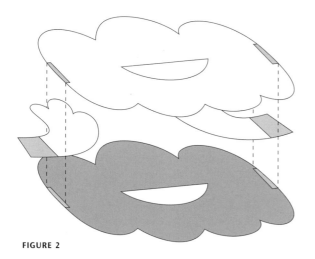

FIGURE 2

8 Pin the tooth pattern to two layers of your contrast fabric. Trace the pattern onto the fabric and cut it out. Sew the tooth together, leaving the end open for turning and stuffing. Invert and stuff the tooth.

9 Pin the tooth in place to one side of the mouth. Stitch the half of the mouth where the tooth is, and knot off. Stuff the rest of the cloud, and then finish sewing the mouth shut. Okay, another hug.

10 On to the eyes! Thread an embroidery needle with the embroidery floss and knot off the end. Enter the cloud through a seam where you can tug the knot through. Use a running stitch to embroider a gentle curve from end to peak to end. Tie off and snip. Repeat for each eye on both sides. Finally, add the tear. Use sewing thread in a color that matches the tear to appliqué the tear in place.

11 Now give Llorie a hug. You've been sticking her with pins and needles, and it made her very sad.

Variations

Creatures made using simple, reversible forms are like having two plush in one. After all, we all have a happy face and a darker side...

Green Monster

Green Monster eats up to 17,000 times his own body mass in a day and never gains a pound. Long, sinewy arms allow him to deftly snare his meals. He prefers to snack on cast-off furniture on street curbs, and unattended zoo animals, such as the benevolent giraffe.

Stuff You'll Need

Green Monster template (see page 120)

2 pieces of light green felt

Piece of dark green felt

Piece of black felt (for hands, feet, and hair)

Tissue paper (to trace and embroider face)

Pencil

Embroidery needle

Black embroidery floss

FINISHED PROJECT SIZE AS PICTURED IS 6¹/₂ X 4 INCHES (BODY ONLY).

How to Create Green Monster

1 Enlarge, copy, and cut out the pattern pieces. Pin the patterns on the felt, and cut the number of pieces indicated on each individual pattern. The seam allowance is included in this pattern.

2 Trace the monster face onto the tissue paper and pin it to the felt face piece. Embroider with either a chain or back stitch. Gently tear away the paper to reveal the face.

3 Time to work on the limbs. Match each arm together with its hand, and each leg together with its toes. For each arm and leg, sandwich the hand or toes in between the front and back pieces of material. Sew around the edges, beginning at the area where the hand or toes attach. Stuff with the polyester fiber as you go.

4 Put the head together by pinning the face and the triangular side panels together, and stitching along the sides. Stitch the back side of the head to the triangular panels, and then stitch in Monster's black hair to the top of his head.

5 Now you can work on the body by pinning the front body piece to the square side panels and stitching them along the sides. Add Monster's back,

making sure to reverse the direction of the body piece from the way it is in the front, and stitch. Put the bottom piece in place, pinning the finished legs in each corner. Stitch everything in place.

6 Stitch the arms to roughly the middle of the square side panels.

7 Stuff the bottom of Green Monster and pin the head piece to it. Stitch the head to the body, filling with more stuffing as needed.

71

DESIGNER: **LIZETTE GRECO**

Sprinkles

He's got a silky smooth, neopolitan cranium and waffly-good quilted feet.
Adorned with fancy sprinkles and a cherry on top, he is SOOO delicious!
Guaranteed not to melt, but we can't say he won't melt your heart!

Stuff You'll Need

Sprinkles template (see page 121)

Pink, white, and brown satin

Iron

Sturdy tan fabric (old khaki pants work great)

Dark brown thread

Black felt

Fabric glue

2 googly eyes

40 black or brown bugle beads

Hot glue and glue gun

Red pom-pom, 2-inch diameter

FINISHED PROJECT SIZE AS PICTURED IS 6¹/₂ X 9 INCHES.

How to Create Sprinkles

1 Enlarge, copy, and cut out the pattern pieces. Cut out two strawberry pieces from pink satin, two vanilla pieces from white satin, and two chocolate pieces from brown satin. These will form the neopolitan cranium.

2 Pin the long side of one strawberry and one chocolate piece together, right sides facing each other, then stitch together.

3 Pin a vanilla piece to the other side of the strawberry piece in the same fashion. Stitch together, and press flat. You now have one side of the cranium.

4 Make the back of the cranium the same way, but reverse the chocolate and vanilla.

5 Trace the legs twice onto a piece of sturdy tan fabric, but do not cut them out yet. Create the waffle texture of the ice cream cone legs by stitching a grid onto the legs with dark brown thread.

6 Now cut out the legs and, with right sides facing each other, pin each one to the cranium pieces along the long, straight edge. Stitch the legs to the cranium and press flat.

7 Cut two 1¹/₄-inch circles out of black felt, and glue them onto the front panel—one on the vanilla side and one on the chocolate side. Glue a 1-inch googly eye onto each of the felt circles.

8 When the glue is completely dry, pin the two body panels to each other, right sides facing together.

9 Stitch around the body, leaving about a 1¹/₂-inch opening in the chocolate area for stuffing (the darker fabric will hide the hand-stitching better). Be sure to backstitch at the beginning and end of the seam for strength.

10 Turn inside out, stuff with polyester stuffing, and hand-stitch the opening closed.

11 The bugle beads serve as sprinkles. Cut a long piece of thread, a few feet long, to stitch on the sprinkles. Start by making a small stitch on the body and tying a knot. String on a bead and stitch a short distance away to where the next sprinkle will be placed. Repeat until the whole face is covered with sprinkles. Tie a knot securing the end of the thread. Thread the ends of your thread through the body to hide them.

12 Hot-glue a 2-inch red pom-pom to the top of Sprinkles's head.

DESIGNER: **JENNY HARADA**

Randall

Once a celebrated quantum physicist, Randall one day stumbled upon the formula for marshmallow Peeps. He traded his scientific reputation for celebrity status— gaining fortune, but losing the esteem of his academic colleagues. He now spends his days calling himself on his cell phone and leaving messages so he feels popular.

Stuff You'll Need

- Fleece for body
- Faux fur or felt for eyebrows
- Black embroidery floss for eyes (size 25 doubled on your needle is ideal)
- Felt for teeth
- Felt for hair
- Tailor's chalk

FINISHED PROJECT SIZE AS PICTURED IS 8¹/₂ X 8 INCHES.

How to Create a Randall Blobby

1 Using the photograph as a guide, draw or trace, and then enlarge and cut out the pattern pieces.

2 Fold the fleece fabric in half, pin the pattern to the fabric, and cut it out. Now you should have two body pieces.

3 To make the eyebrows, cut two rectangles out of the faux fur.

4 Lay one of the fleece body pieces right side up and pin the fur eyebrow pieces on the body. Stitch the fur pieces onto the single layer body. After stitching, pull your threads to the backside with a needle, knot them, and snip. This leaves a clean front.

5 Using embroidery floss, stitch two eyes underneath the eyebrows. To make the teeth, fold a piece of felt in half. Stitch three teeth onto the folded felt, then cut them out (figure 1).

6 For the hair, fold two pieces of felt in half. Pin down. Trace the hair patterns onto the folded felt with tailor's chalk. Don't cut yet! Stitch along the chalk line, creating double-thickness hair pieces. Cut out after stitching (figure 2).

7 Now you are ready to put Randall together. Place the back body piece right side up. Place your three felt teeth on the fleece with the rough edges along the seam edge. Do the same with the two hair pieces. Place the front body

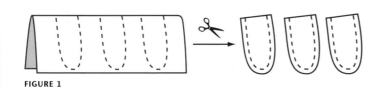

FIGURE 1

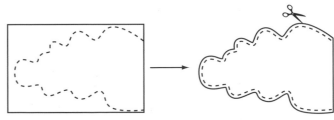

FIGURE 2

DESIGNER: **MARIA SAMUELSON**

piece right side down on top, sandwiching the teeth and hair (figure 3). Pin the pieces together, making sure to catch the teeth and hair in the pins. Stitch along the edge with a 3/8-inch seam. Leave approximately 2 inches unsewn along the backside for turning your Blobby right side out and stuffing it. Back-tack at the start and end of stitching.

8 Trim and clip on the curves, corners, and between the toes. Be careful not to clip any seams! Turn Randall inside out and stuff.

9 Hand-sew the stuffing hole closed. Stitch in the seam to hide your stitching, knot your thread when done, and then bring the thread ends back into the blobby with your needle. Bring the needle out again after an inch or two, then snip threads close to the Blobby body. This hides the threads inside Randall.

FIGURE 3

Woolies

The Woolies are monsters who, while not terribly bright, are renowned for their soft, woolly fur and cheery dispositions, making them excellent companions—and in a pinch, comfy pillows. They like to play group games and sing camp songs loud and off-key. Inevitably, they blame each other for cheating at a game or singing out of tune, and a raucous fight ensues. Just as your mom warned, it's all fun and games until someone loses an eye.

Stuff You'll Need

2 sweaters in 2 different colors (see Creating Felted Wool Fabric on page 9)

Felt

Large-eyed embroidery needle

Embroidery floss (for mouth, fangs, and missing eye)

2 buttons for eyes (one larger than the other)

Ribbon or trim for belt

FINISHED PROJECT SIZE AS PICTURED IS 8½ X 14 INCHES.

DESIGNER: **LORI KAY LUDWIG**

How to Create a Woolie

1 Using the photograph as a guide, draw or trace, and then enlarge and cut out the pattern pieces. Pin each pattern securely to your selected fabric so it lies flat. Cut out the pattern pieces, leaving a ¼-inch seam allowance around each. When cutting out a piece that forms a front and back, remember to flip the pattern piece over before pinning and cutting the second piece.

2 A Woolie monster is sewn from four separate pieces. Placing right sides together, pin together the top and bottom pieces that form the Woolie's front by pinning at the straight edge. Do the same with the back pieces. The feet should be facing in the same direction as the top of the head.

3 Join the two colors by sewing a seam across the pinned area. Open the front and back pieces and match them up in order to double-check that you have the right sides together, and that all the limbs will be aligned when the Woolie is assembled.

4 With right sides together, pin the front and the back of the monster body together. Sew around the edges, leaving at least a ¼-inch seam allowance. Leave a small opening just to either side of the crotch area for stuffing. Be sure to backstitch as you finish, so the sewing doesn't come undone as you stuff.

5 Stuff firmly from the head to the arms, down to the feet, then finish up with the torso. Sew the opening closed using a ladder stitch.

6 Use a blanket or whipstitch to stitch on the oval felt face. Embroider the Woolie's mouth, fangs, and an "X" for his eye. Sew on the two buttons for the other eye.

7 If desired, create a stylish belt for your Woolie by attaching trim using a blanket stitch.

Variations

The Woolies take great pride in their fashion sense. Some are more conservative, sporting bold solids, while others step out in snazzy stripes and flashy belts. Personalize your Woolie by embellishing him with vintage trim, a patterned sweater, or whatever strikes your fancy. Heck, check out Crazy Cuzin Woolie (he's the one with horns and sprouting flowering eyes)!

Moopy Bunny

Moopy Bunny looks like your sweet and innocent girl next door, but as soon as you turn your back she is pinching the last chip in the bowl, or even worse, the cherry on top of your ice cream.

Stuff You'll Need

- Fluffy gray felt
- Tailor's chalk
- Red patterned fabric (for skirt)
- Light beige/cream felt
- Dark brown embroidery floss
- Embroidery needle
- Another different red patterned fabric (for ears)
- Striped cotton fabric

FINISHED PROJECT SIZE AS PICTURED IS 6 X 12 INCHES.

How to Create Moopy

1 Using the photograph as a guide, draw or trace, and then enlarge and cut out the pattern pieces.

2 Pin the four corners of two pieces of gray felt together. Make sure the material is a few inches larger in size than your pattern. This will become Moopy's body form. Trace the pattern onto the felt using tailor's chalk. Mark a 2-inch opening under Moopy's upraised arm to show where you'll insert the stuffing. This will also serve as a guide for where you should start and stop sewing.

3 Re-pin the felt just inside of the traced shape. Trim around the pattern, leaving an approximate 1/4-inch seam allowance.

4 Cut out the skirt pieces. Pin the top of the skirt fabric facedown against the bottom of Moopy's body, and sew a simple straight line to attach. Repeat with the other body and skirt pieces.

5 Cut the round face out of light-colored felt, and sew into place. Use the brown embroidery floss to stitch the X's in Moopy's eyes and then her mouth. Make sure that you're stitching them to the right side of the felt (the skirt pattern should be facing out).

6 Cut out Moopy's ears—two pieces from felt and two from red fabric. Sew the fabric to the felt with the fabric side facing down. Turn the ears right side out.

7 Do the same for the legs using the striped fabric, and lightly stuff.

8 Pin the body form with right sides together. Sew around the outline of the body form, starting and stopping at the labeled openings. Remember to tuck the legs and ears inside the body form, leaving enough overhang to sew them into the seam. Pinning them in place makes things easier.

9 Trim away any excess felt around the sewn body form, and snip into corners so they don't bunch. Turn the body form right side out.

10 Stuff the body beginning at the bottom, and then gradually fill toward the top. Hand-stitch closed.

DESIGNER: **CARLY SCHWERDT**

Onimushi

Onimushi are often mistaken for very large bugs, but they're actually very small, grouchy monsters. They are notorious troublemakers, so if you create one, the best thing to do is to keep it inside a large glass canning jar. (Don't forget to poke holes in the top or it will turn blue!)

Stuff You'll Need

Onimushi template (see page 122)

Felt in several colors of your choice

Ballpoint pen

Fusible web material

Iron and ironing board

Embroidery floss in colors of your choice

Plastic beads for stuffing (optional)

FINISHED PROJECT SIZE AS PICTURED IS 5 X 9¹/₂ INCHES.

How to Create an Onimushi

1 Enlarge, copy, and cut out the pattern pieces.

2 Lay one piece of fabric on top of another, and pin the body pattern to them. Cut out the body.

3 With a ballpoint pen, trace the facial features, details, and arms onto an iron-on, fusible web product. Leaving at least ¹/₈ inch outside of your pen line, trim out the pieces of fusible web and lay them onto the desired fabric.

4 Following the manufacturer's directions, iron the pieces on the fabric. Do not let the iron get too hot, as felt will melt!

5 Cut out all the shapes along the pen line. Peel off the paper backing from all the pieces, leaving the fusible web. This is a good time to sew any details on these pieces.

6 Arrange the eye parts, mouth, and stomach shape on the body, and iron, following the manufacturer's

83

directions. It is often easiest to iron on only one or two pieces at a time, to ensure they don't shift accidentally.

7 Lay the arms on a slightly larger piece of fabric (same color) and iron them together. Trim to the same size. Repeat for the antennae and wings. Using a stiff fabric for the wings should allow you to prop up the finished Onimushi, so that it stands on its own!

8 Follow the same procedure for the claws, but before ironing the two sides of the claws together, put the tip of the arm between the two pieces so that they will be fused.

9 By now your bug should look pretty buggy, so it's time to sew!

Arrange the bug so that the front sides are facing each other, marking the places you need to leave open for the claws, antennae, and for stuffing. Sew around the edge of the fabric, and when you're finished, turn it right side out again.

10 Stuff with plastic pellets to give the plush some weight, or use polyester fiberfill stuffing—or both. Now just sew the opening closed, and Onimushi is ready to wreak havoc!

Variations

Like the dwarfs in Snow White, these little guys each project their own unique personality. Your choice of eye treatment, and the selection of an upturned grin or a fierce grimace will determine whether your Omnimushi uses his powers for good or evil.

Demented
Dogs

Demented Dogs are a new plush breed of canine. They're a lot like other dogs, only not quite as clever. Tell them to "sit" and they just stand there, tell them to "fetch," and they just stand there! The only way to get these crazy canines to do what they're told is to tempt them with their favorite food—sausages!

Stuff You'll Need

Demented Dog template
(see page 123)

Tailor's chalk

Fabric

White felt

2 buttons

Old pair of tights or nylons

Thread

FINISHED PROJECT SIZE AS PICTURED IS 9¹/₂ X 9 INCHES.

How to Create a Demented Dog

1 Enlarge, copy, and cut out the pattern pieces. Pin the patterns to your fabric, and cut around them.

2 Once you have all the pieces of your dog cut out, begin making the body by sewing the four feet into place on the body with a zigzag stitch set to 0.5 "stitch length."

3 Pin one body and one inside leg together, making sure the feet you have just sewn are on the inside (figure 1). You will do all the sewing on the inside, and then turn it inside out later.

4 Now sew around the legs with an ordinary straight stitch, leaving the top

DESIGNER: **RUSS HENRY**

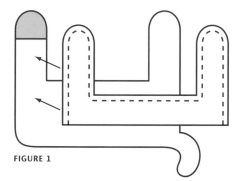

FIGURE 1

edge open. Do the same with the other body and inside leg pieces. Remember that the inside leg will be sewn onto the opposite side of the body (figure 2).

5 Pin the two bodies together, on top of one another, making sure the "inside legs" are on the inside (figure 3).

6 Next sew from point A (the edge of the inside leg) to B (the dog's bum), as indicated in figure 3.

7 All you need to do now is turn your dog inside out. Stuff him with polyester fiber, making sure you stuff all the way to the tail. Hand-sew the gap together, from X to Y (figure 4). And that's it for the body!

8 To make the head, pin the two sides of the head together (right sides facing) and sew around them with a straight stitch, leaving an unstitched space in order to turn the head inside out.

9 Turn the head inside out. Stuff, and then hand-sew the opening closed.

10 Attach the eyes. Use a ladder stitch to attach the head to the body.

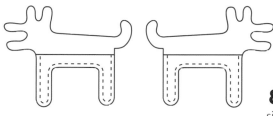

FIGURE 2

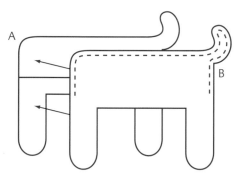

FIGURE 3

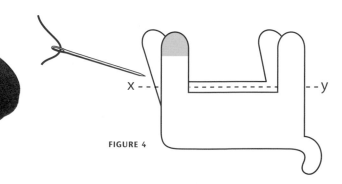

FIGURE 4

Making Sausages

1 Take an old pair of tights or nylons and cut a piece approximately 8 inches long and 4 inches wide. Fold the piece in half, widthwise, and sew a line approximately $5/8$ inch from the open edge.

2 Cut off the excess material and turn inside out to make a tube. Next, tie one end of the tights with thread, leaving a little "sausage casing" end.

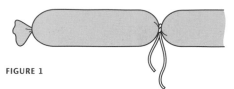

FIGURE 1

3 Now take a small amount of stuffing (about the size of a ping pong ball), and push this to the tied end of the tube. Tie some more thread above this wadding to make one sausage (figure 1).

4 Repeat this process until you have enough sausages, then simply cut off the rest of the tube, leaving another "sausage end."

Variations

Except when fighting over sausages, Demented Dogs are an agreeable bunch and like to travel in packs, so you'll want to make several. Whether solid, spotted, or multi-colored, these mutts make great watchdogs, devoted companions, and quirky conversation pieces.

Earless
Elephant

The Earless Elephant is a rare species, numbering at about one (1). Often the subject of great speculation, the earless elephant hears by picking up vibrations with its trunk. It flies through the air buoyed by love, and if it should happen to eat a bug by mistake, it deposits its unintended snack safely back into the wild with a gentle cough.

Stuff You'll Need

Earless Elephant template
   (see page 124)

Fleece (for body and tail)

Patterned cotton fabric for belly

2 cups of rice or lentils (for weights)

Scraps of fleece for feet and snout

4 large paper clips (for feet)

Tissue paper (to mark embroidery
   work on snout)

Embroidery needle

Black embroidery floss

Note: The trunk of this elephant tilted it forward, so weights are in the legs to keep the elephant's trunk in the air instead of touching the ground.

How to Create an Earless Elephant

1 Enlarge, copy, and cut out the pattern pieces. Pin the body pattern to the fleece and cut out two pieces, leaving a 1/4-inch seam allowance. Note that the end of the snout on the back body piece is longer than on the front body piece.

2 With right sides together, sew the body of your elephant together from the top of the trunk to just above

DESIGNER: **LIZETTE GRECO**

where the tail will be attached. Sew the underside of the trunk all the way to the opposite side of the opening for the tail.

3 Cut out the piece that goes between the legs. Fold and pin it to the front and back pieces forming the belly. Sew it in place leaving the bottom sides, where the legs attach, open.

4 Stuff the elephant to give shape to the trunk, head, and half of its body.

5 Cut out two tail pieces. Place right sides together, and sew around all the sides except the end that attaches. Turn right side out, stuff, and sew closed.

6 Cut out four "weight" pieces. Sew two weight pieces together to form a sack. Leave an opening so you can fill it with the necessary weight. Repeat with the other two weight pieces. Fill both sacks with rice or lentils until they are almost,

but not quite, full. Sew closed, and insert a weight horizontally between the front and back legs on each side of the elephant. Add stuffing to the body, and arrange so that there are no gaps between the weights and the rest of the body. Pin the bottom edges of the belly piece closed so the weights don't come out. Set aside.

7 Cut out four back and four front leg pieces. For each leg, place two pieces together and hand-sew around all the sides except for the portion where the foot attaches to the body—leave that open for stuffing. Fold a large paper clip in half, wrap a little stuffing around it, and insert it into the foot. Add more stuffing as needed, and sew closed. Repeat the same procedure with each foot.

8 Pin each foot in place, and hand-stitch them to the bottom of the elephant's body, closing that area, and leaving the weights secured in place.

9 Cut the snout piece out of tissue paper, and pin to a scrap of fleece. Cut around the tissue paper. Embroider air holes on the snout circle, and then gently tear away the tissue paper, leaving the embroidery. Sew the snout onto the end of the trunk, in the area indicated on the pattern, sealing the area. Add stuffing as needed.

10 Add a little stitch for the pupil, and sew the eyes in place. Sew the tail in place.

Grégoire's gaping mouth belies his vocation as a talented mime. On weekday afternoons he can usually be found performing outside the Pompidou Center, much to the delight of locals and tourists alike. He does leave early on Fridays in August to enjoy long weekends at his country villa, so plan accordingly.

Stuff You'll Need

Grégoire template (see page 125)

Tailor's chalk or water-soluble fabric marking pen

Fake fur or thick fleece fabric (for body)

Ruler

Fleece fabric (for pocket mouth)

Cotton bias tape

2 different colors of felt (for eyes and ears)

2 buttons (for eyes)

FINISHED PROJECT SIZE AS PICTURED IS 7 X 8 INCHES.

How to Create Grégoire

1 Enlarge, copy, and cut out the pattern pieces. Using tailor's chalk or a water-soluble pen, trace the body pattern onto the wrong side of your selected fabric. Use a ruler to trace a line where the mouth will be. Cut out two body pieces, leaving a ¼-inch seam allowance.

2 With the right sides together, pin both pieces of fabric together. Sew all around the outline of the body form.

3 Cut along the mouth line being careful to cut only the front of the body, not through both layers of fabric. Turn body inside out through the mouth opening.

4 Cut out and sew together two pieces of fleece for the pocket mouth using the same method as for the body. Cut along the pocket's opening just as you did for the body.

5 Stuff your creature, making the ears, legs, and "forehead" areas harder than the rest of the body so that enough room will remain for the pocket and any future contents.

6 Turn the fleece pocket right side out and place it inside the body, aligning the creature's mouth with the pocket's opening. Add more stuffing if the body feels too soft. Hand-stitch the edges of Grégorie's mouth and pocket opening together.

7 Cut two pieces of cotton bias tape ½ inch larger than your creature's mouth. Fold in the extremities and hand-stitch them onto the creature to form the lips.

8 Cut felt pieces for the ears and eyes, and hand-stitch them in place. Sew on the buttons for eyes.

Variations

Gregoire has the wanderlust, and likes nothing better than to tag along on your daily excursions. But he's no mooch—you'll find him to be quite accommodating. With the addition of a simple strap, he'll keep your cell phone, M3P player, or other life's necessities secure and readily accessible.

93

DESIGNER: **ROSA POMAR**

Bryan

Bryan is a big guy, but has delicate hands, albeit fingerless ones. He takes his security job at the Louvre very seriously, and if necessary, he uses an intimidating glare to silence rowdy schoolchildren. His penchant for the works of Canaletto is only surpassed by his love for cannoli.

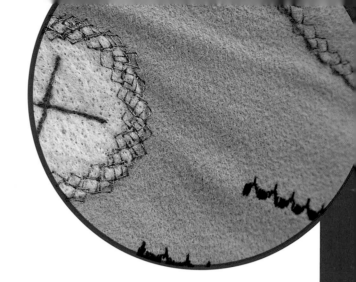

Stuff You'll Need

Bryan template (see page 126)

Fabric of your choice

Felt

Plastic eyes

FINISHED PROJECT SIZE AS PICTURED IS 10 X 26 INCHES (BODY ONLY). ARMS ARE 19 INCHES AND LEGS ARE 10 INCHES LONG.

How to Create Bryan

1 Enlarge and copy the pattern pieces. Pin the pattern pieces to the appropriate fabric, and cut out the number indicated on the pattern.

2 With right sides together, sew the arms, legs, nose, and ear pieces together, leaving the top of each open.

3 Firmly stuff the arms and legs, leaving 1½ inches unstuffed at the open end.

4 To make Bryan's rotund belly, you need to sew four darts. With right sides of the fabric together, fold the material on the dotted lines indicated on the pattern, and pin the dart in place. Stitch the dart on the dotted lines sewing from the widest end toward the point. Leave a 4 to 5-inch tail on the thread, and hand-knot the thread at the point of the dart.

5 Now is the time to apply Bryan's details that give him his rugged good looks. Use an overlocking or narrow zigzag stitch to sew on Bryan's nose and all the felt pieces like the eyes, belly, nipples, 5 o-clock shadow, and then his lips and belly button.

6 To create Bryan's comb-over, start near the top of his head and sew a vertical length. Backstitch, and then drag the thread to the opposite side of the head, sewing another vertical length parallel to the first. Repeat this process at least 15 times, moving down Bryan's forehead.

7 Use decorative stitches to stitch on Bryan's forehead wrinkles, chest hair, beard stubble, and stretch marks.

8 Place the front body piece faceup and lay the ears, arms, and legs in position, facing inward. Make sure they overlap the seam enough to get sewn in securely. Place the back body piece on top, with the right side facing down. Pin and sew all the way around Bryan's body, leaving an area unstitched so you can turn Bryan right side out. Reinforce the stitching around the arms, legs, and ears.

9 Attach the plastic eyes.

10 Turn Bryan's body right side out and stuff it until quite firm. Bryan is a toy in his mature years—he is meant to look paunchy. Sew the stuffing opening closed.

95

DESIGNER: **BECK WHEELER**

You may wonder what types of individuals channel their deepest thoughts, inside jokes, unadulterated creativity, and wacky vision into the spawning of edgy, attitude-endowed plush toys. And you may ask yourself, "What makes them do it? Are they possessed? Obsessed? Were they potty trained too early?"

Surprisingly enough, they are probably much like you. No super-powers or insanity run in the family...just an insatiable urge to create— whether that creation be a mixed-media piece of art, fiber wearable, or a plush alter ego. One common thread is that there's nary an idle hand in the bunch, as most have been zealously creating and inventing all their lives.

Come on then, turn the page and

Meet the Designers

Rachel Chow & Jason Carpenter of

Creature Co-op is the creative cooperation between Rachel Chow, Jason Carpenter, and our friends and family. We started Creature Co-op in 2004 as a hobby to create cute yet dark plush friends with strong personalities. Our first creature was a pitiful and slightly scary two-piece felt Voodoo doll with a hand-stitched heart. Our love for the Voodoo doll encouraged us to make more complicated creatures based on animals. Soon Bunny, Porco, Klong, and Julio were born. They were joined soon after by Crazy Cat and Klops. This was our starting lineup. We continually

develop new creatures to add to our group of stuffed friends. We draw inspiration from everything around us: people we know and love, people we don't, imaginary friends, pets, animals, books, cartoons, and pop culture.

All Creature Co-op products are proudly handmade with loving care in the great U.S.A. We strive to make the Creature Co-op experience creative and fun for all who encounter it.

We live, work, and play in Los Angeles, California.

To see more Creature Co-op designs, visit **www.creatureco-op.com**.

Creature Co-op

Lizette Greco

Kids' stories are a good place to find inspiration. A little friend of ours told us about the snails that crawled up the wall of her house. I started drawing snails and writing a little story to go with it. Then I made a bag with a snail appliqué on it for her fifth birthday. Since it was fun to do, I tried a few more drawings, but wanted to personalize my kids' gifts to their friends, so I turned to their drawings and saw a lot of potential for embroideries, appliqués, and why not—softies.

Turning my children's drawings into toys seemed a natural thing to do. I was thinking the other day that I enjoy my sewing because I like to show off my kids, and this is a sort of indirect way to say "look at what my kids drew today (and in a softer, sort of whispering voice), and look at what I did with it."

To see more of Lizette's designs, visit **www.lizettegreco.com**.

Jenny Harada

Hello, my name is Jenny Harada, and I make stuffed animals. I started sewing at the wee age of seven. My mom taught me how to use her sewing machine, and I started out making doll clothes. By age 10 I graduated to stuffies; 23 years later, I am now making my own line of wacky, whimsical, and colorful creatures. You can always find me creating them 'round the clock at my home studio in Ohio, where I hang out all day with my cute little baby, cute husband, and cute doggie. I strongly believe in recycling, so many of my chosen materials include old sweaters, coats, jeans, and even my father's old shirts! Then I throw brightly colored shaggy fur into the mix, and it's just pure delight. My current line of creatures has been available on my website since 2004, and I am always adding new designs.

To see more of Jenny's designs, visit **www.jennyharada.com**.

102

Grace Montenar

My Spasmodica character line was originally developed as mascots for a now defunct webzine called POP!sicle that I co-published with a friend several years ago. After POP!sicle melted away, the creatures were given new life in the form of plush dolls because it seemed a shame to keep them in the 2-D world where they were born.

In the beginning, I couldn't resist the urge to create something just to see if anyone would be interested in it. Now I continue because my day job as a senior graphic designer has zapped the creativity out of me, and Spasmodica helps to infuse it back into my life. I also like to play store.

I find inspiration in everything around me that is good, bad, interesting, dull, silly, happy, sad, cheap, expensive, smart, dumb arsy, ergonomic, musical, and childlike, but I'm especially enamored with inanimate objects bearing faces. My wonder nieces, Allison and Gabby, are also a constant source of inspiration.

As for Harry, (pictured on page 39), let's just say he has chosen an alternative lifestyle. To read more about Harry and his friends, visit **www.spasmodica.com**.

Rosa Pomar

I live in Lisboa, Portugal, and started making cloth dolls because of the wonderful experience I had as a child playing with the ones my mother made for me. After I became a mother myself, I wanted to make some dolls for my daughter. As soon as I started, it was obvious to me that I wasn't going to stop making them any time soon. Since I didn't want my daughter to have so many that she'd lose interest in them, and I had received a lot of positive feedback from people who visited my weblog, I decided to start selling them. I like working with natural fibers such as

wool, linen, silk, and cotton. Many of my dolls are made from a fantastic blend of wool and cashmere—very soft. My decorations and appliqués consist mostly of vintage cotton lace and embroidered ribbon that I have collected over the years.

To see more of Rosa's designs, visit **www.rosapomar.com**.

Photograph by João Cardoso Ribeiro

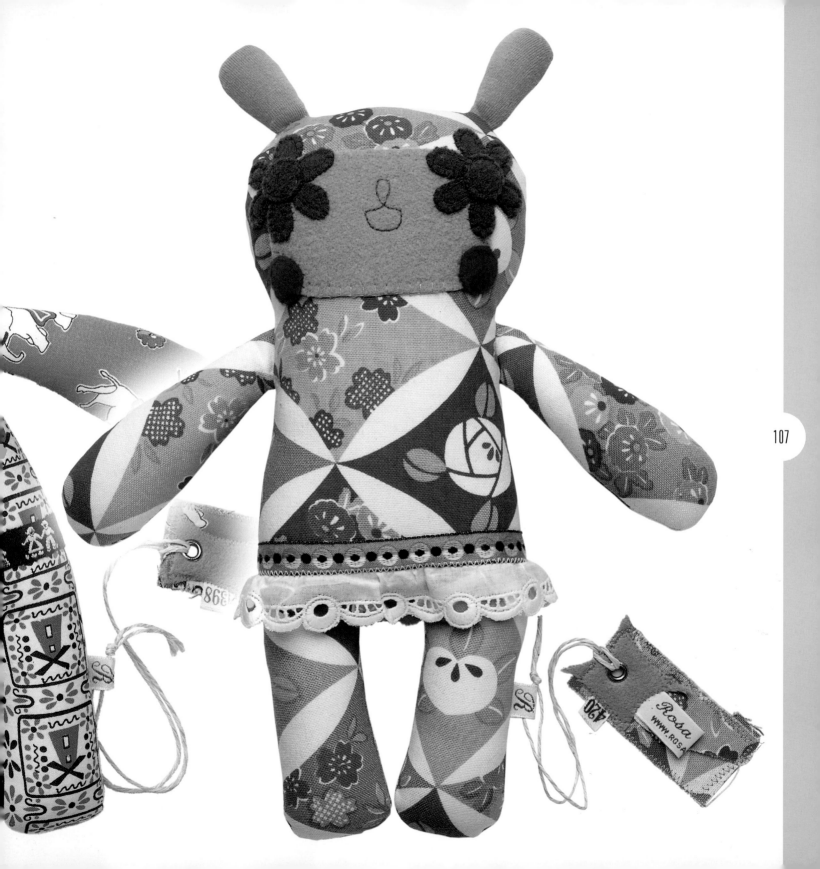

Beck Wheeler

I am a German-born artist who studied sculpture and jewelry in Auckland, New Zealand, before moving to Australia in 2000. I then went on to study painting and illustration in Melbourne, where I now work as a freelance illustrator/toy designer.

My first toy was made in 2001 in an attempt to bring to life a comic strip I was working on. The comic strip soon got buried under an ever-growing pile of soft creatures, and what started as an occasional pastime grew into a full blown passion for toy making. In 2004, I launched my label, Kissy Kissy Toys. Kissy Kissy Toys are made out of a medley of wool felt, retro fabric, and odds and ends found in secondhand boutiques.

In a world where everything is mass-made, mass-produced, and mass-consumed, I aim to make toys that reek of being handmade. I rarely work from a pattern, so each toy has its own unique look and personality.

To see more of Beck's designs, visit **www.kissykissytoys.com**.

Designer Biographies

ASHLEY BAKER

Ashley Baker is the brainchild of Adorned, her own design company. She makes scarves, handbags, Neko Fuzzlings, and other vintage accessories that she currently sells in boutiques in the U.S. and Europe. Ashley is also one of the founding members of Seattle's premier craft show, Urban Craft Uprising. She lives in an old, funky house with her sweetie Sam, and their two fuzzy kitties. Ashley finds her inspiration in artwork and nature, especially flowers, and her eye is always on the lookout for different uses of color and patterns. Ashley's designs can be seen at **be-adorned.com**.

JESSICA CROKER

Jessica Croker was born in Boise, Idaho, and received a BFA in art (with an emphasis in printmaking) from Utah State University. She currently resides in Ohio, where she spends her time reading books, singing songs, playing with toys, and dreaming up projects she can fit into her career as a mother of three little kids. See more of Jessica's work at **seedpodbooksandart.com**.

BERTHA CROWLEY

Bertha began her artistic career young in life. Window shades, walls, and furniture provided an ideal canvas for the young girl, but fortunately her parents decided to keep her anyway. Nowadays, Bertha enjoys creating in her spare time to relieve the crippling drudgery of her software-related job. She lives in Massachusetts with her husband, Matt, and their two cats, Ripple and Cassidy, from whom she draws much of her inspiration. You can find her work at **karmakitties.com**.

DARREN FRISINA AND ESTHER WAIN

Based in Perth, Western Australia, Esther Wain and Darren Frisina enjoy combining their talents to design and create quirky and slightly twisted plush toys. Designing under the collective name of Fiendish Toys (**www.fiendishtoys.com**), their aim is to design totally unique and individual toys for people who want something out of the ordinary. Esther and Darren gain their creative inspiration from cartoons, high chocolate consumption, and the weird and wonderful animals that already exist on our planet.

RUSS HENRY

Russ Henry is a graphic artist/image-maker from the north of England. He is currently based in Bristol studying illustration. Russ likes making things, sewing, sawing, knitting, painting, and drawing. He combines all these crafts with a simple, fun graphic style. Skulls, knitwear, and monsters are often depicted in his work, which has been exhibited in various exhibitions across the U.K. Some of the things that influence Russ are old magazines/annuals, pattern design, graffiti, children's books, and rock 'n roll.

DAVID HUYCK

David Huyck grew up in the suburban flatlands north of Chicago. He and his brothers played with Legos, drew from Ed Emberly's how-to-draw books, watched a lot of cartoons and Muppets, and read "The Far Side" and "Calvin and Hobbes" obsessively. David still loves to read comics, watch cartoons, and let his imagination run rampant with his pen. Lately his imagination has also taken control of his mom's old sewing machine. His work comes from playing, experimenting, inventing, and happy accidents. His images and toys always have a story to tell, but what may seem innocent on first impression might not always be so. Watch your back. See more of David's work at **bunchofmonkeys.com**.

LORI KAY LUDWIG

LK Ludwig is an artist living in Pennsylvania with two very clever monsters who serve as a constant source of inspiration and laughter. Her work may also be seen in *Artful Paper Dolls*, (Lark Books, 2006); *Altered Books, Collaborative Journals and Other Adventures in Book Making*, (Quarry Books, 2003), as well as other publications.

AMY PROFF LYONS

Amy Proff Lyons creates whimsical folk art, combining vintage and contemporary components whenever possible. Her work is charming and often tongue-in-cheek. Amy's work has been featured in a handful of exhibits and publications. Amy's inspiration comes from her little boys' wide-eyed imaginations, as well as anything old and well-loved. She lives and works in Denton, Texas, with her husband Lynn, and their two little boys, Logan and Caleb. See more of Amy's work at **aplcreations.com**.

JEN RAREY

Jen had her formal training at The Columbus College of Art & Design in her hometown of Columbus, Ohio, and then moved to Kansas City to work for a big greeting card company as an illustrator and art director. She enjoys experimenting with a variety of media including printmaking, photography, web design, and plush. Jen's work is inspired by music, pop culture, vintage and contemporary character design, and all animals—but especially her two bratty cats, Atom and Gypsy. Her work has been featured in a multitude of exhibitions and in *Super 7* magazine, *Creative Review* (UK), and the *War of Monsters* book (France). For fun she collects vinyl monster toys and children's books, studies Japanese, and watches campy monster movies. Find out more about Jen and her work at **www.studio-rama.com**.

MARIA SAMUELSON

Maria Samuelson is a resident of Greencastle, Indiana, where she sews Blobbies: small, plush, goofy-looking creatures. Her Masters degree in Theater History and Criticism is currently hibernating under stacks of fleece and felt. She is a die-hard fan of Hawaii Five-O, and dreams of one day making a Steve McGarrett Blobby. Blobby ambassadors have been sent to shows far and wide. She works closely with her husband, Christopher, when designing the Blobbies. They credit Mr. T, Go-Bots (the underdogs to the Transformers), gross words for food (like cheese log and chicken plank), and the music of DV Cassette Club as direct influences upon their work. To see Maria's latest Blobbies, visit **blobbyfarm.com**.

CARLY SCHWERDT

Carly lives in Adelaide, Australia with her two inspirations in life, husband Chris, and daughter Lily. She teaches children art in her quaint little studio, where she also runs a design business and shop, Nest Studio. Nest Studio sells handmade products for children (or big kids) that have been made by crafty bloggers from around the globe as well as other Australian designers. Carly's own line of toys and children's products can be found in her shop and in other shops around Australia. Nest Studio holds the bi-annual toy exhibition Morphe. Visit **neststudio.com** for more of Carly's work.

KATE SUTTON

Kate Sutton is an illustrator based in the UK. Her simple line drawings and strange plush creatures come from a love of old children's books, knitting, trees, and car boot sales. Other influences include all things handmade, old food packaging, and 1970s' rock. Because brown is her favorite color, she tends to use it a lot in her work (she thinks sometimes maybe too much). Other recurring themes in Kate's work are birds, trees, and lots and lots of hand-drawn fonts. See Kate's latest work at **sleepycow.com**.

LEYA WILLIAMS

Leya Williams, also known as Curious Bird, is the creator and nimble fingers behind the online boutique curious-bird.com—a quirky place to purchase handmade items and vintage finds for people and their nests. Having a fondness for vintage fabrics, photo booths, birds, and renegade gardening, Leya resides in North Carolina with her partner, Dustin, and two very sleepy cats, Mortimer and Motown. Visit **curiousbird.com** to see Leya's latest designs.

Templates

Enlarge pattern pieces to your desired size.

Hexapus

PAGE 36

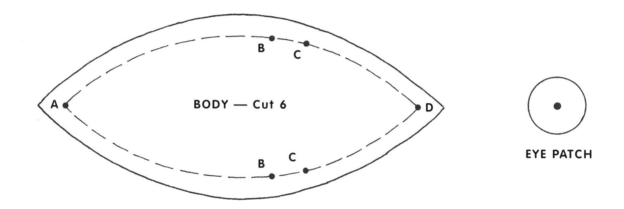

BODY — Cut 6

EYE PATCH

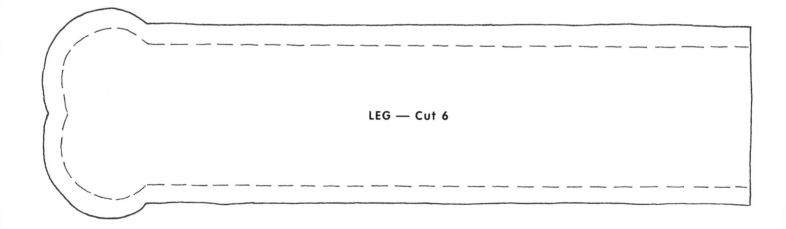

LEG — Cut 6

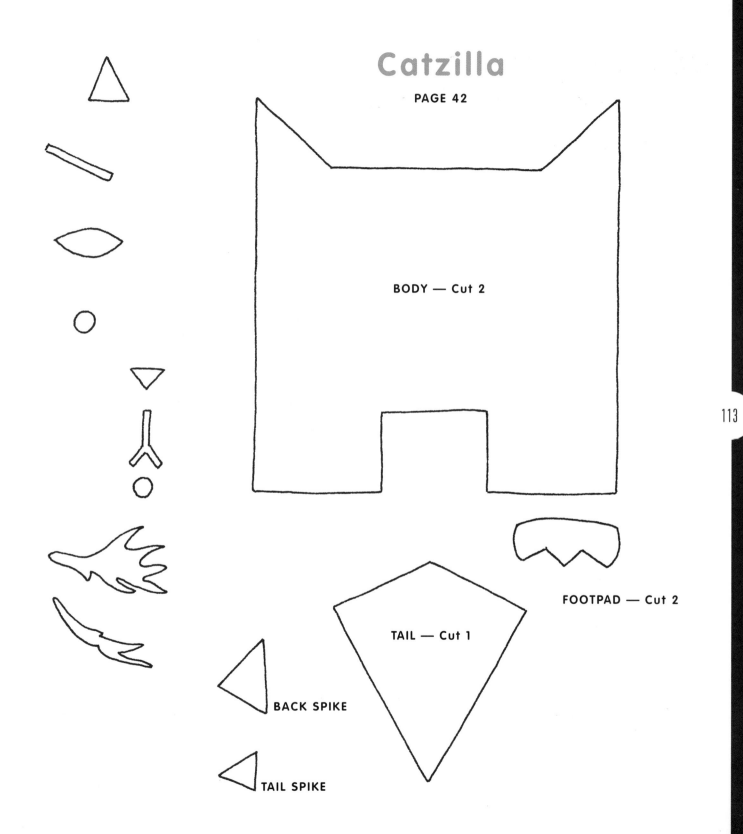

Catzilla

PAGE 42

BODY — Cut 2

FOOTPAD — Cut 2

TAIL — Cut 1

BACK SPIKE

TAIL SPIKE

113

Plucky

PAGE 46

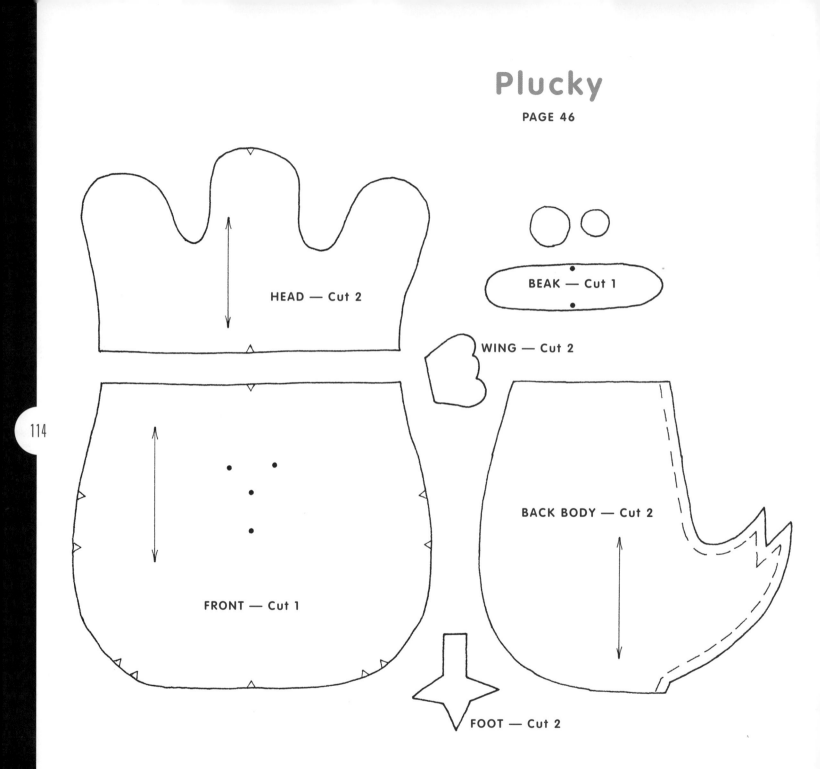

HEAD — Cut 2

BEAK — Cut 1

WING — Cut 2

BACK BODY — Cut 2

FRONT — Cut 1

FOOT — Cut 2

114

Pig/Duck

PAGE 48

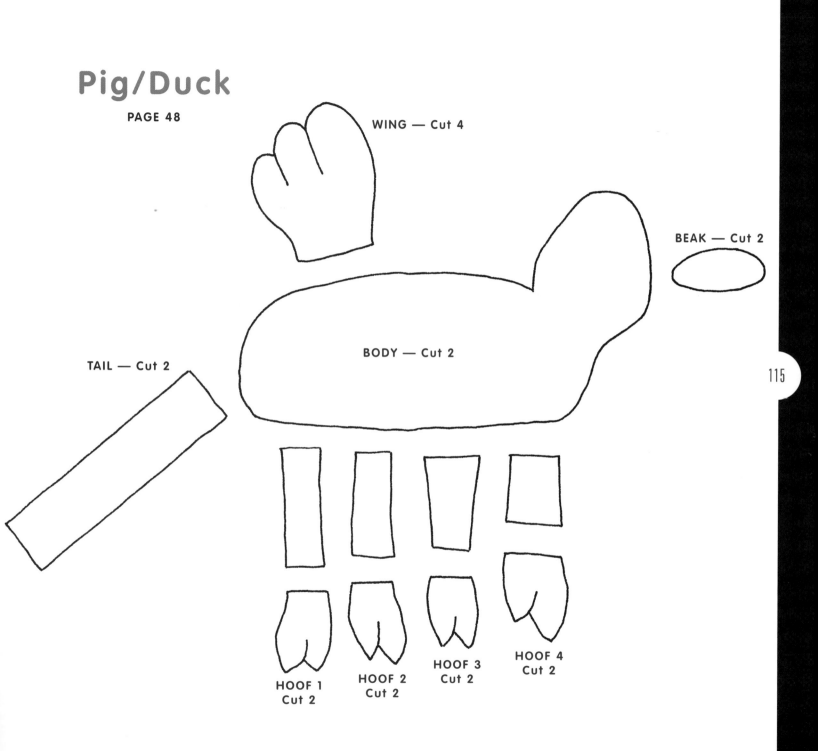

WING — Cut 4

BEAK — Cut 2

BODY — Cut 2

TAIL — Cut 2

HOOF 1 Cut 2

HOOF 2 Cut 2

HOOF 3 Cut 2

HOOF 4 Cut 2

Candy Apple Neko

PAGE 50

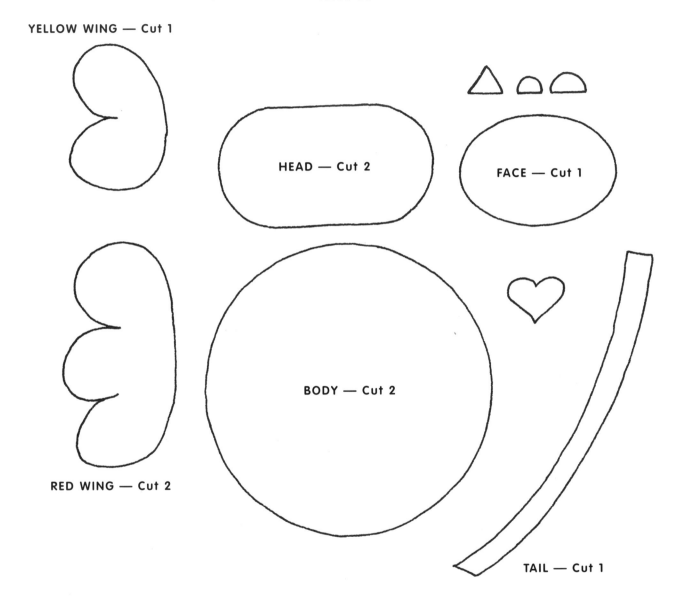

YELLOW WING — Cut 1

HEAD — Cut 2

FACE — Cut 1

BODY — Cut 2

RED WING — Cut 2

TAIL — Cut 1

Apple Tree

PAGE 56

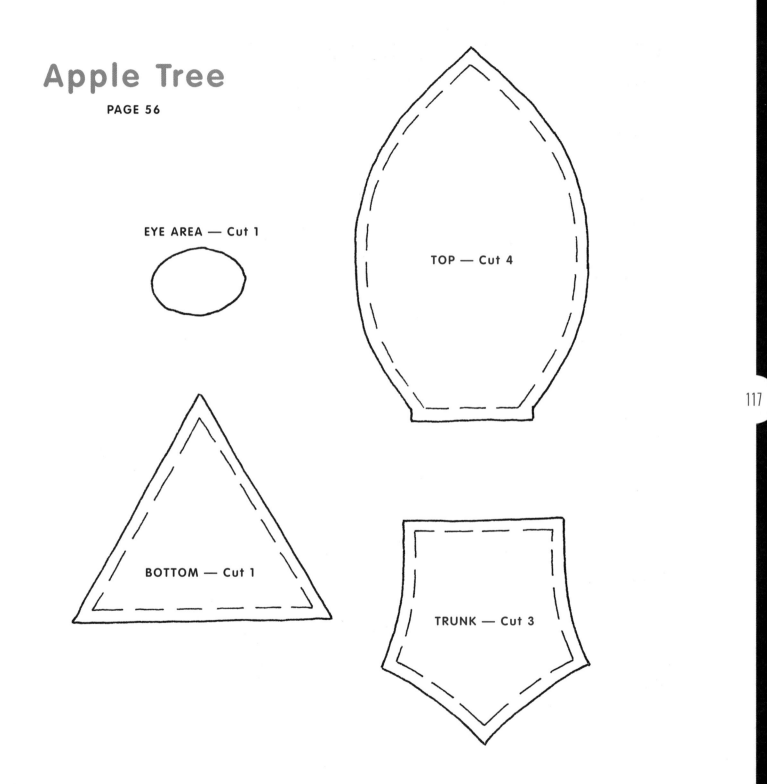

EYE AREA — Cut 1

TOP — Cut 4

BOTTOM — Cut 1

TRUNK — Cut 3

Gremlin

PAGE 58

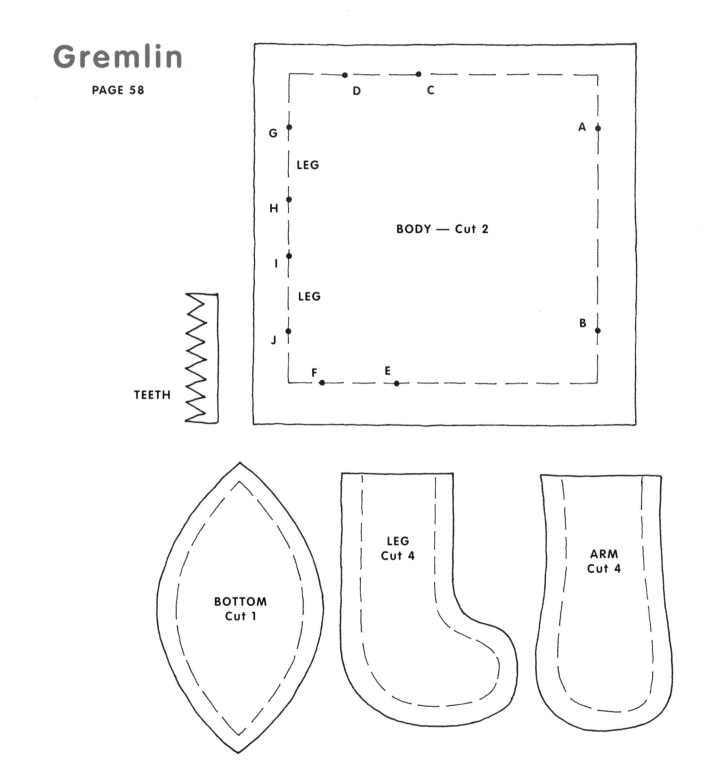

G

LEG

H

I

LEG

J

TEETH

D   C

A

BODY — Cut 2

B

F   E

BOTTOM
Cut 1

LEG
Cut 4

ARM
Cut 4

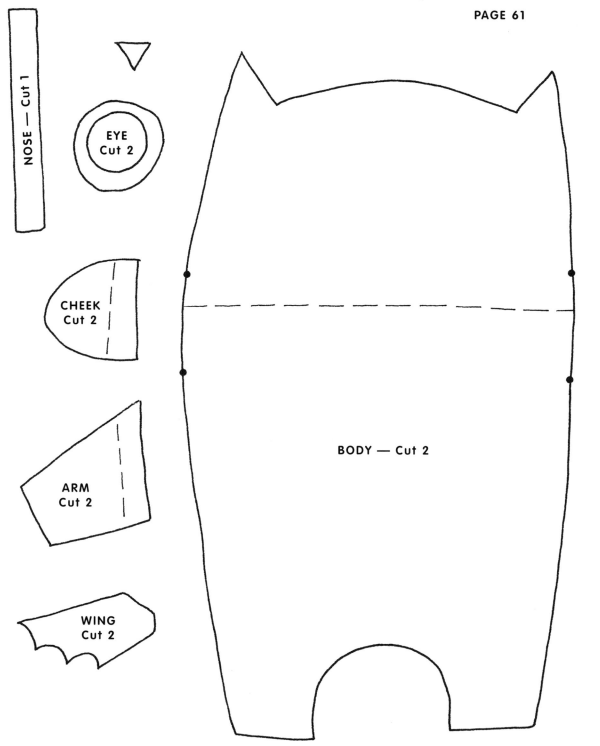

NOSE — Cut 1

EYE
Cut 2

CHEEK
Cut 2

ARM
Cut 2

WING
Cut 2

BODY — Cut 2

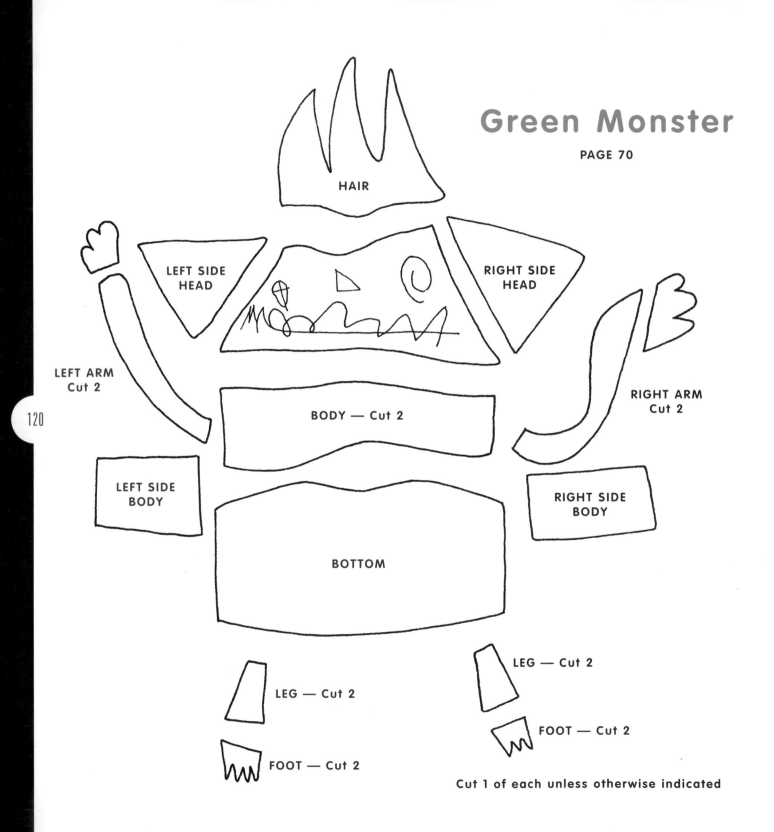

Green Monster

PAGE 70

HAIR

LEFT SIDE HEAD

RIGHT SIDE HEAD

LEFT ARM
Cut 2

RIGHT ARM
Cut 2

BODY — Cut 2

LEFT SIDE BODY

RIGHT SIDE BODY

BOTTOM

LEG — Cut 2

LEG — Cut 2

FOOT — Cut 2

FOOT — Cut 2

Cut 1 of each unless otherwise indicated

STRAWBERRY
Cut 2

VANILLA
Cut 2

CHOCOLATE
Cut 2

Sprinkles

PAGE 72

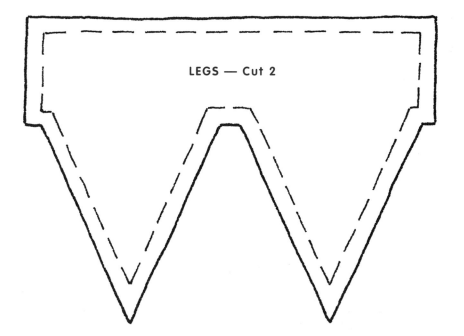

LEGS — Cut 2

Onimushi

PAGE 82

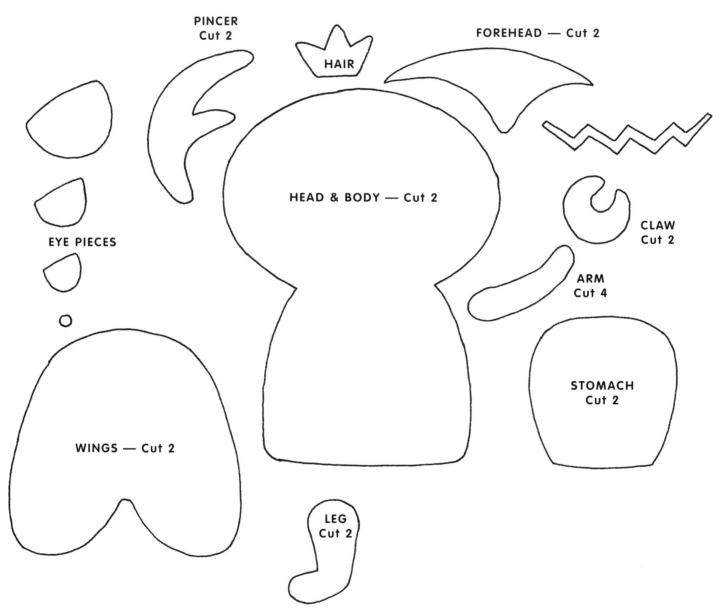

PINCER
Cut 2

HAIR

FOREHEAD — Cut 2

EYE PIECES

HEAD & BODY — Cut 2

CLAW
Cut 2

ARM
Cut 4

STOMACH
Cut 2

WINGS — Cut 2

LEG
Cut 2

122

Demented Dogs

PAGE 85

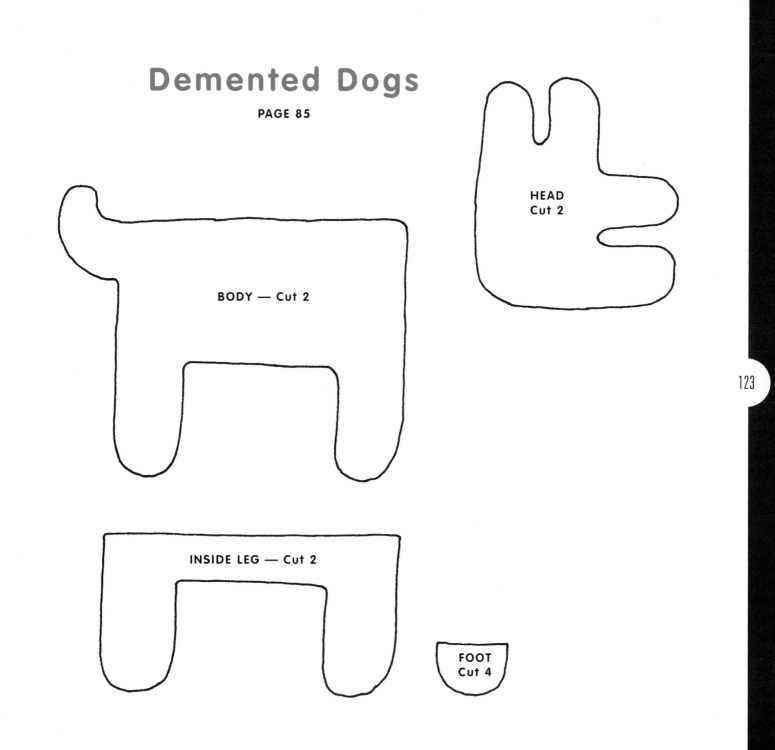

HEAD
Cut 2

BODY — Cut 2

INSIDE LEG — Cut 2

FOOT
Cut 4

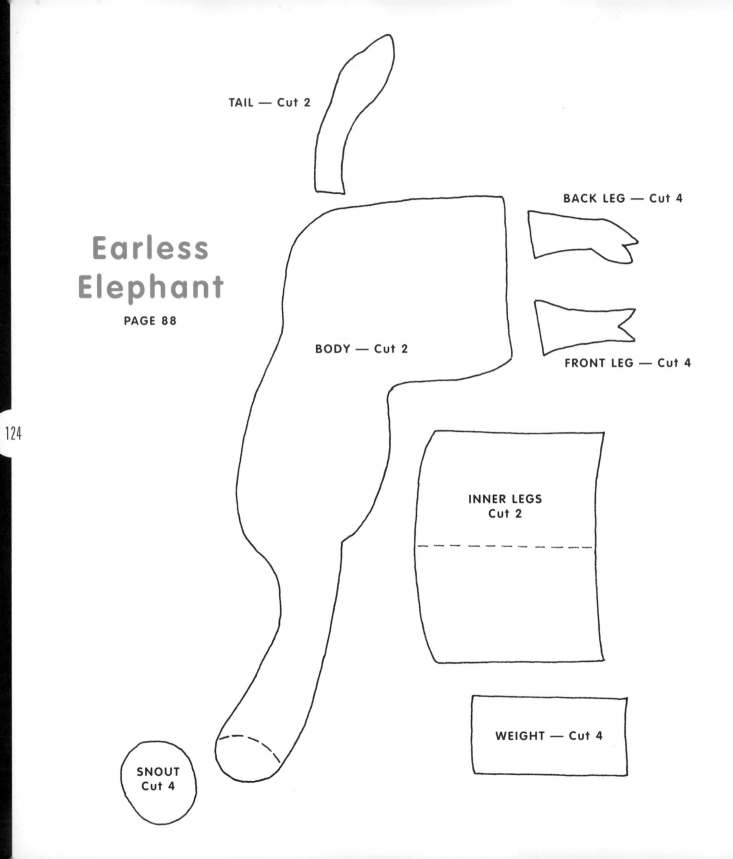

TAIL — Cut 2

BACK LEG — Cut 4

Earless Elephant

PAGE 88

FRONT LEG — Cut 4

BODY — Cut 2

INNER LEGS
Cut 2

124

WEIGHT — Cut 4

SNOUT
Cut 4

Grégorie

PAGE 92

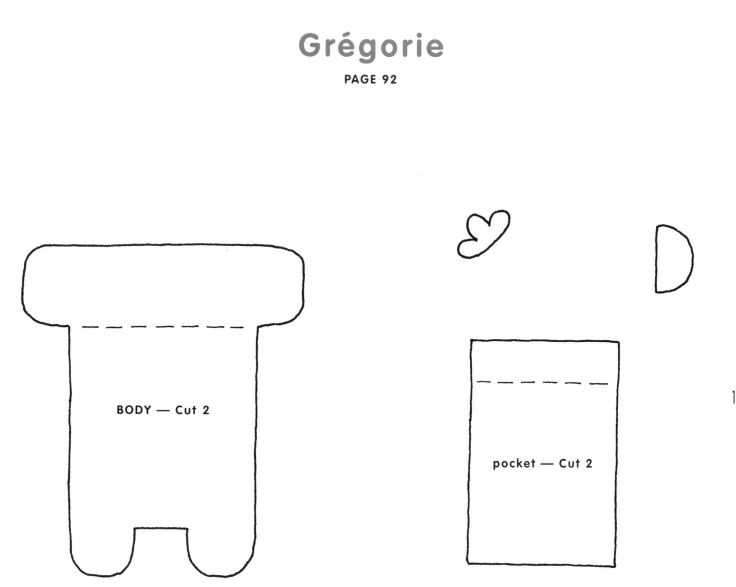

BODY — Cut 2

pocket — Cut 2

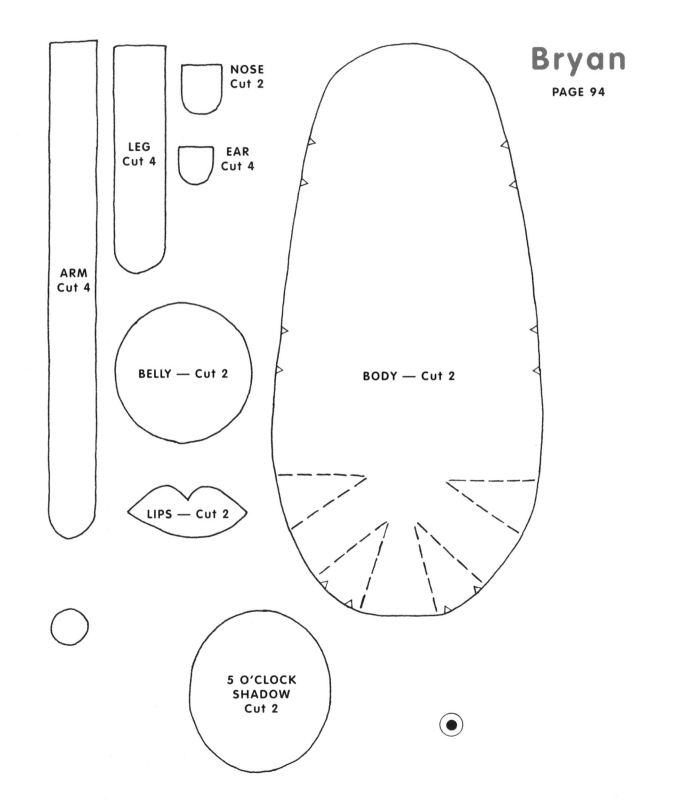

Bryan

PAGE 94

NOSE
Cut 2

LEG
Cut 4

EAR
Cut 4

ARM
Cut 4

BELLY — Cut 2

BODY — Cut 2

LIPS — Cut 2

5 O'CLOCK
SHADOW
Cut 2

126

Acknowledgements

I want to offer a heartfelt and resounding thanks to:

Lori Kay Ludwig for sharing her knowledge regarding Creating Felted Wool Fabric, (featured on page 9), enabling plushers everywhere to make legions of felted plush (and Woolies) of their own.

Also to all the incredibly talented and off-beat designers who focused their enthusiasm and gray matter into creating plush that make people smile. Kudos to you all!

METRIC EQUIVALENTS

Inches	Centimeters	Inches	Centimeters
1/8	3 mm	12	30
1/4	6 mm	13	32.5
3/8	9 mm	14	35
1/2	1.3	15	37.5
5/8	1.6	16	40
3/4	1.9	17	42.5
7/8	2.2	18	45
1	2.5	19	47.5
1 1/4	3.1	20	50
1 1/2	3.8	21	52.5
1 3/4	4.4	22	55
2	5	23	57.5
2 1/2	6.25	24	60
3	7.5	25	62.5
3 1/2	8.8	26	65
4	10	27	67.5
4 1/2	11.3	28	70
5	12.5	29	72.5
5 1/2	13.8	30	75
6	15	31	77.5
7	17.5	32	80
8	20	33	82.5
9	22.5	34	85
10	25	35	87.5
11	27.5	36	90

Index